THIRTEEN WORTHIES

THIRTEEN
WORTHIES

LLEWELYN POWYS

With a Preface by
VAN WYCK BROOKS

REDCLIFFE
Bristol

**First published in 1923
by the American Library Service, New York**

**This edition first published
in 1983 by Redcliffe Press Ltd,
14 Dowry Square, Bristol 8**

© *Eve Elwin*

ISBN 0 905459 59 8

Printed in Great Britain by
Villiers Publications Ltd.

This small book is dedicated in admiration and devotion to the last of the Thirteen Worthies, whose footfalls still, by the Grace of God, indent the turnpike roads, the honeysuckle lanes, the flinty ewe-cropped downs of the ancient county of Dorset.

PREFACE

GENERATIONS of Harvard freshmen will recall the scorn with which Professor Kittredge used to inveigh against the misapplication of the word " quaint." Perhaps he still does so: it was the association of the adjective with Chaucer's jocund image that especially provoked, as I remember, those indignant shakings of the old word-master's lion-like head. Chaucer was a man of the world and his idiom was an idiom of the world—that was the drift of the professorial argument. It was the most infamous of errors to think of him in terms that might be applied to some rustic wiseacre, some provincial spinster of a bygone age.

No doubt this word quaint has been sadly abused. Strictly speaking, it is as little appropriate as any of the other adjectives that rise so easily to our lips when we think of the worthies—eight or ten of them at least—of whom Mr Powys writes in these engaging essays. We need a word which, like a Chinese ideogram,

7

conveys a complex mental picture and touches in a flash the springs of the five senses, a word that suggests, among other things, the ruddy skins, slightly shrivelled, the toughness and viscosity, the pungent flavour of rare country apples that have been laid away for the winter.

I am the freer to use this figure because Mr Powys' worthies are all so redolent of the vegetable kingdom: their veins seem to flow as much with the sap of trees as with the blood of animals and (on occasion) the ichor of angels. How firmly planted they appear to be in the fat soil of those old-world meadows and river bottoms of which their writings, so sweet and so bitter, might almost be taken for a direct expression. Various as were the parts they played in life, and far as some of them wandered in the world, their poetry and their wisdom, as Mr Powys shows us, were fruits of the long infancy, the profound, productive inertia of that abundant rural life of old times.

Nothing could be more charming than the slow pleasure with which Mr Powys lingers over the memory of these grave, gentle, honest, lusty and curious men. He delights in letting them go their own way, in following their meandering minds, in tracing their idiosyncrasies and their humours. He has, we gather, something in common with them : he shares their belief perhaps, the belief expressed by a certain French philosopher, that one should carefully cultivate one's faults. For the rest, Roundhead and Royalist are alike to him so long as they are men of letters. Moreover, he is the best of tasters when it comes to these well-matured literary vintages. The papers on Izaak Walton, Bunyan, Chaucer, and Montaigne are certain to revive in many a mind many an old affection. With Nicholas Culpeper and Tom Coryat, on the other hand, most readers will make their first acquaintance in the savoury pages of this little book. But one and all, exalted or obscure, these worthies live again and live worthily, in the happy cadences of Mr Powys' prose.

VAN WYCK BROOKS.

CONTENTS

NOTE

The following essays have already appeared either in " The Freeman," " The Dial," " The North American Review," or " The Forum," and are printed here with the kind permission of the editors.

GEOFFREY CHAUCER

GEOFFREY CHAUCER

THERE is something curiously appropriate in the fact that Geoffrey Chaucer sprang from a family of wine merchants. Such a profession may happily enough be associated with a poet whose turn of mind, grateful to the senses, was tempered also with a proverbial gaiety. It is probable that the actual name Chaucer is derived from the word Chaufecire or chafe-wax; a chafe-wax being the officer in the Court of Chancery whose business it was to prepare the large wax seals used for royal documents. This may also be considered apposite. For, after Shakespeare, who is there in English literature who would seem to have underscored the varied manifestations of life with so emphatic and catholic a sanction?

Indeed, there is in the genial aplomb of Chaucer's verse something that leads us to surmise that this well-constituted courtier and man of affairs was blessed with a lust for existence as unflagging as it was unequalled. From the year 1357 when, a lad of seventeen, he was provided by his good benefactor—the Lady Elizabeth—with a paltok (or cloak) and a pair of red and black breeches, till the year of his burial in Westminster Abbey, we may well believe that he contemplated with the deepest personal satisfaction every aspect of life, happy or sad, moral or immoral, that was presented to his sly and earthbound intelligence.

Geoffrey Chaucer belongs to those poets for whom the actual, sweating, visible world is sufficient. No heavenly fanfare was able to divert his downcast eyes from the hedgerows, fish-ponds, and ale-stakes of his familiar environment. His feet are firmly planted in meadow soil, and the heels of his pointed, mediæval shoon have ever upon them honest, grass - smelling dung from the parkland enclosures of the Home Counties. Not even Wordsworth has succeeded as well as Chaucer in conveying to the reader that particular thrill that comes each year in England with the first days of spring. It is no evasive thing. It has none of the intangibility of the rainy seasons in tropical lands. It is a thrill that is palpable. It is as apparent to the young, clean-hoofed steers in the growing meads as to the newly arrived cuckoo, who, all the morning long, from shrouded elms, with careless orange throat, shouts wantonly across the mild, soft-scented air. The little round roots of the celandines are conscious of it as, also, are the opening daisies. Daisies! it was not for nothing that Chaucer selected that brave, contented, little English flower to be his especial favourite. If anybody should desire some comfortable token by which he could at any time be reminded of the quality of Chaucer's poetry, let him take up a handful of daisies from a lawn freshly mown, and inhale their simple odour. With such an innocent bouquet against his nostrils, a bouquet so drugged with sunshine and earth-mould, surely he must catch the very flavour and indefinable aroma of the *Canterbury Tales*.

It is a fact that the more familiar one is with Chaucer's poetry, the more one comes to realise that probably no other portion of the earth's surface save the sod of England would have been in accord with his sturdy temperament. In such an island, however, there is no scene or sensation that he could not, and does not, welcome. As Dryden long afterwards

17

said of his poetry : " Here indeed is God's plenty."

Every chance incident, every stray event, every flower and animal and bird, caused him, as has been so admirably pointed out by Mr Aldous Huxley, to " shout for joy." He is capable of deriving satisfaction from the simplest scenes : from the ungainly deportment, for instance, of one of those roguish, self-indulgent monks, so familiar a sight in the country-side of his day—

"   . . . Like Jovynian,
Fat as a whal, and walken as a swan "

—or from the quite ordinary spectacle of a mortal labouring under the heat of the summer sun.

" A docke-leef he had under his hood
For sweat, and for to kepe his hed from hete.
But it was joye for to see him swete."

Not a fowl of the air but he remarks upon it and appreciates its peculiarities—the " schrychynge owls," the " false lapwing, ful of treacherie,"

" The swalowe murdrer of the beess male
That maken honie of floures fresh of hew."

18

His composition has no taint of " moralic acid " about it. For better or for worse he is content to take the world as he finds it. Natural goodness, natural spontaneous piety, he is well able to appreciate, but naught will persuade him that good can come from any restrictions that outrage the laws of nature. In the following stubborn lines he puts his point of view plainly enough :—

" But God it wot, no man so strong can
    prove
As to destroy a thing, the which natúre
Hath naturelly set in a créatúre ;
Tak any bird, and put him in a cage,
And do all thyne entent and thy corráge
To foster it tenderly with meat and
    drynke
And with alle the deynties thou canst be
    thinke,
And keep it alle so kindly as thou may :
Although his cage of gold be never so
    gay,
Yet hath this bird, by twenty thousand
    fold,
Lever in a forest, that is wylde and
    cold
Gon eten wormes and such wrecchidnes."

Indeed, one finds, quite continually in his writings, the frankest recognition and avowal of every pleasure that is to be derived from the senses. In such matters, as often as not, he caused the "Wyf of Bathe," a woman naturally broad of mouth, to act as his spokesman. Ideals of chastity, she asserts, are all very well for those

> "that wolde lyve parfytly
> But, Lordyngs, by your leve, that am not I
> . . . .
> I nil envye no virginitie."

"Round of schape" and "elvish by his countenance," we are justified in supposing that Chaucer himself was not one to forgo any of those temptations which may be regarded as man's rightful heritage. Without doubt he was, to use Sir Thomas Urquhart's favourite language, an "Honest Cod," and one who, to his great content, could inhale the early morning air, as he set out in the direction of Canterbury, with the delightful April sunshine glancing down upon the tiles, and cornices, and swinging weather-vanes of Southwark, five hundred years ago!

How essentially, how intimately English the famous poem is! So admirably has he managed to interweave the various tales with the encounters and casual dialogues of the actual wayfaring that, long before Broughton on Blee is reached, we have come to feel that we ourselves might be one of the company, so vividly is the motley troop brought before our imagination as it ambles forward, up hill and down dale, across the broad hop-bearing acres of Kent!

What excellent matter is contained in the *Tales* themselves. The most Rabelaisian of them make good reading. Who can forget, for example, that scene in the raftered room of the old Mill house at " Trompyngtoun nat fer fro Cantebrigge " ?—

" For at an hool in schon the moone
    bright."

And what description of a young girl could be more realistic and living than that of Alisoun? With one audacious stroke he likens her limber body to that of a weasel, and when one recalls the swift, supple movements of that particular animal, could anything be more provocative? Her voice is like the sound of a swallow " chiteryng on a berne," while her appearance is lovely as a pear-tree in

21

early bloom; she is softer to the touch than the wool on the back of a sheep, and she is fragrant as a heap of apples laid away in hay or heather.

There is sufficient evidence, however, to prove that Geoffrey Chaucer's attitude to women was not always qualified with so gracious an appreciation :

" Ther nys, i-wis, no serpent so cruel,
When men trede on his tail, ne half so fel,
As woman is, when sche hath caught an
    ire."

After the Host of the Tabard Inn had listened to the tale of the sweet gentleness of Prudence, the wife of Melibeus, he is made to exclaim with heartfelt intensity :

       " As I am a faithful man,
And by the precious corpus Madryan.
I hadde rather than a barel ale
That good woman my wyf had herd this
    tale.
For she is no thing of such pacience
As was this Melibeus wyf Prudence.
By Goddes boones! whan I bete my
    knaves,
She bringeth me forth the grete clobbed
    staves,

And crieth ' sley the dogges every one !
And breke of them the bak and eek the
bone ! ' "

Chaucer evidently felt in sympathy with
that old saying which declares that a
woman should be absent from her home
only three times during her life—" when
she is christened, when she is married,
and when she is buried." He recognised
what dangers lie even in the mere possession of fine clothes !

" And if the cattes skin be sleek and gay,
   She will not dwell in house half a day
   But forth she will, every day be dawet
   To show her skin an gon a caterurawet."

Are we to attribute such passages to a bitter
personal experience? Was his Philippa,
with whom for so many years he was wont
to share the pitcher of wine that he had
daily from the King's cellar, something
of a thorn in the old man's flesh? Certain
well-known lines would seem to indicate as
much.

It is at any rate quite clear that " the
ancient and learned English poet " was
not easily to be fooled, was in fact fully
awake to what takes place in " This wyde

23

world, which men seye is round." He regarded with complacent amusement every anomaly, every extravagance! He does not in the least resent the impostures practised by the Church. There is not a grain of malice in his description of the Pardoner and his merry ways :

" Then peyne I me to strecche forth my
      necke,
And est and west upon the people I bekke,
As doth a pigeon, sytting on a loft."

He is not in the least put out by the fact that the rascal goes through the shires with the shoulder - bone of " an holy Jewes shepe " under his cassock; a relic which he declares would cause any well water into which it was dipped to cure the farmer's flocks of " scabbe " and " wormes " :

" By this gaude have I wonnen every yeer
An hundred mark, synce I was pardoner."

Nor does the following outrageous avowal seem at all to disturb him :—

" For myn entent is nought but for to
      wynne,
And no thing for correccion of synne.

I rekke never at their burying
Though that their soules go black-
   berrying."

Dangerous as was any display of levity
or unbelief in those days, he cannot altogether refrain on certain occasions from re-
vealing the inherent scepticism of his own
mind :

" A thousand tymes have I herd men telle,
That ther is joye in heven and peyne in
   helle ;
And I accorde wel that hit is so ;
But natherless, yit wot I wel also,
That ther nis noon dwelling in this
   countree,
That either hath in heven or helle y-be."

His descriptions of the changing seasons are always admirable. Has the spirit
of Christmas time, one wonders, when
" frostie fieldfares " are abroad everywhere on the chilled ploughed lands, ever
found happier expression than in these
lines ?—

" The bitter frostes with the sleet and reyn,
   Destroyed hath the green in every yerd.
   Janus sit by the fyre, with double berd,
   And drinketh of his bugle-horn the wyne ;

25

Before his stant the braun of tusked
  swyne,
And ' Nowel ' cryeth every lusty man."

But celebrate as he may the delights of
the " bugle-horn," as the son of a vintner,
he cannot refrain from volunteering some
shrewd advice about ·the white wine of
Lepe which in his day was to be bought
in Cheap Street, London :

" Of which there ryseth such fumositie
That when a man hath dronken draughtes
  three
And weneth that he be at hoom in Chepe
He is in Spayne, right at the toune of
  Lepe."

Chaucer died in the year 1400 and was
the first of the great English poets to be
buried in that side chapel of Westminster
Abbey which is now known as the Poets'
Corner. His pilgrimage was over at last :
those long years of courtly service ; those
summer nights when it was, as he tells us,
his habit to sleep out of doors ; and his
strange relationship with Cecilie de Cham-
paigne ! There, to this day, " nayled in
his chest," lie the bones of this man who
was to become the " deere maister and

fadir " of so many great writers ; the bones
of this genial man, " jolly as a pye," who,
one may believe, was well content to have
lived in just such a land and in just such
a century :

" But, Lord Christ, when that it remem-
  breth me
Upon my youth, and on my jollite
It tikilith me aboute myn herte-roote !
Unto this day it doth myn herte boote,
That I have had my world as in my tyme."

MICHEL
DE MONTAIGNE

MICHEL DE MONTAIGNE

ON a lichen-covered wall of an ancient
château which for long ages had
stood "amid the fat noonday Gascon
scenery," these words, carved deeply in
the crumbling masonry, were to be read
by the curious for many generations:
"In the year of our Lord 1571, at the age
of thirty-eight, on the last day of February,
being the anniversary of his birth, Monsieur
de Montaigne, long weary of the service
of the Court and of public employments,
while still in his full vigour, betook himself to the bosom of the nine learned
virgins." Could anything have been more
significant of the character, tastes, and
sturdy Epicurean aplomb of the man to
whom they owed their origin?

In every sense that the gracious phrase
implies, Montaigne was first and last "a
good European" and not one inclined to
set aside the true values of life. A generous
lover of leisure, of spiritual and physical
well-being, of curious meditations, of
quaint erudition, he was by no means a

man to suffer his days to slide by unnoticed because of an over-zealous preoccupation with the illusive activities that belong to everyday life. It is said that Montaigne was an eleven months' child, and indeed in his shrewd, slow-moving constitution —so full of a mature sanity—there is something that goes to suggest a longer time in the making than is granted to most mortal men.

He was born in a turbulent and un-settled age, an age as bewildered with difficulties and confusions as is our own, and yet was able to reach to an adjustment with life which for civilised poise has scarcely been surpassed before or since. He was fortunate in his upbringing. He owed his lifelong enthusiasm "for the greatness of old Greek and Roman life" to the eccentric theories of his father, who, while Michel was a child, would have no word spoken in the château, not even by the servants, except it was Latin. In-deed, so thoroughly was the rule kept that a hundred years later certain Latin nouns were found to have lingered on in the mouths of the ploughmen and vine-tenders employed about the eighteen farms that constituted the broad estates of the castle.

32

It has been remarked that another re-
fining influence invaded the spirit of the
sun-tanned, broad-mouthed *seigneur*—his
meeting with Estienne de la Boëtie. It
happened, so it always seemed to Montaigne, " by some secret appointment of
Heaven," and without doubt it did more
than anything else in his life to impart
to his jocund, earth-bound nature a suspicion that there might be, possibly, after
all, abroad in the world an unutterable
something above and beyond what his
eager and insatiable senses saw and felt.
The memory of his dead friend was never
out of his mind. Twenty years later, he
tells us, when he was bathing in the waters
of Lucca, the thought of the irremediable
loss he had sustained by this death swept
suddenly over his soul with unrebated
bitterness. It was the one experience of
his life that perplexed and astounded the
old sceptic, the one experience capable
of endowing his style with a new tone of
passionate inspiration. There is a certain
pathos in observing how rattled and put
about the old egoist was by this tragic and
unexpected revelation—the old red fox
caught at last in the gin of the absolute!
Craftily he scans the familiar landscape

33

of his mind. How could this be? The explanation of this!—what was it? " Because it was he, because it was I " is all that he, the master " idealclast," finds it in him to say.

For the most part, however, he was able to survey the grotesque panorama of human life with a massive and indelible satisfaction. It pleased him mightily to hold discourse with two aboriginals from the New World whom he lit upon in Rouen. They had come, he tells us, " to learn the wisdom of Europe " and were " men of dignity, although they wore no breeches." He liked to note the fact that " tortoises and ostriches hatch their eggs with only looking on them, which infers that their eyes have in them ejaculative virtue," that " Xerxes was a coxcombical blockhead," that " Carneades was so besotted with knowledge that he would not find time so much as to comb his head or to pare his nails," and that there existed a certain nation that fed on spiders—" Yea, made provision of them and fed them for their tables, as also they did grasshoppers, mice, lizards and bats ; and in a time of a scarcity of such delicacies a toad was sold for six crowns, all which

they cook and dish up with several sauces."
It amused him to observe that when the
vines of his village were nipped with
frost "his parish priest presently concluded that the indignation of God is
gone out against *all the human race*."

But his interests were by no means
confined to such objective observations.
There was nothing that diverted him so
much as to mark down his own peculiar
tastes and idiosyncrasies, whether at home
in his cheerful, sunlit tower, or abroad on
horseback, wrapped about in the dark,
threadbare mantle that had belonged to
his father, "because it seemed to envelop
me in him."

"Nobody prognosticated that I should
be wicked, but only useless; they foresaw
idleness, but no malice; and I find it falls
out accordingly.

"I never inquire, when I am to take
a footman, if he be chaste, but if he be
diligent; and am not solicitous if my
muleteer be given to gaming, if he be
strong and able, or if my cook be a swearer,
if he be a good cook.

"For table-talk, I prefer the pleasant
and witty before the learned and grave;
in bed, beauty before goodness.

35

"The generality of more solid sort of men look upon abundance of children as a great blessing ; I and some others think it a great benefit to be without them.

"I love stout expressions amongst gentlemen and to have them speak as they think.

"I love rain and to dabble in the dirt as well as ducks do.

"I give great authority to my propensions and desires. To be subject to the stone and subject to abstention from eating oysters are two evils instead of one.

"I have ever loved to repose myself, whether sitting or lying, with my heels as high or higher than my seat.

"I do not remember that I ever had the itch, and yet scratching is one of nature's sweetest gratifications. . . . I use it most on my ears, which are often apt to itch.

"We have in us notions that are inconsistent and for which no reason can be given ; for example, I found radishes first grateful to my stomach, since that nauseous, and now again grateful.

"At the little jerks of oars, stealing the vessel from under me, I find, I know not how, both my head and my stomach disordered.

36

" 'Tis indecent, beside the hurt it does to one's health and even to the pleasure of eating, to eat so greedily as I do. I often bite my tongue and sometimes my fingers, in my haste.

" To the end that even sleep itself should not so stupidly escape from me, I have formerly caused myself to be disturbed in my sleep, so that I might the better and more sensibly relish and taste it.

" I have never put myself to great pains to curb the desires by the which I have found myself beset. My virtue is a virtue, or rather an innocence, which is purely random and accidental."

From these and similar utterances what a vivid picture is evoked of the genial, philosophic old aristocrat. His short, thick-set figure, tough and individual as one of his own gnarled vine-stumps, is never out of our sight as we review the various events of his life. There he stands superintending the construction of the lighthouse at Bordeaux for the better direction of the mariners returning from that New World which had so intrigued his imagination ; there he sits, goose-quill in hand, composing the letter in which he proffered his resignation from the mayoralty of the city, for no better reason, forsooth, than the personal apprehension that he felt with regard to the plague. "For my part, I am of the mind that if a man can by any means avoid danger, though by creeping under a calf's skin, I am one that would not be ashamed of the shift."

We see him on his travels observing how ill-favoured were the faces of German women, buying a new fur hat at Augsburg, or rating a Swiss tavern-keeper because his table was ill provided with crayfish! We see him at Rome attending Christmas Mass, or walking the streets, which through his reading were as familiar to him as those of Paris, impatient sometimes of the Renaissance buildings which cluttered up the monumental foundations that were so dear to his heart. They resemble, he thinks, the martins' and jackdaws' nests that adhere to the shattered fragments of the churches in France which had been brought to ruin by the ravages of the Huguenots.

Two volumes of his " Essays " were found in his trunks and fell into the hands of the ecclesiastical censor. He was brought to task by Pope Gregory. He himself willingly enough condemns them before-hand, out of hand, "if so be anything should be found in his rhapsodies contrary to the holy resolutions and prescriptions of the Catholic Apostolic and Roman Church into which I was born and in which I shall die," and then returns to France to publish from the safe retreat of his castle the very passages to which exception has been taken. He visits the unfortunate Tasso in his convent at Ferrara, and in the papal library peers curiously at the writing of St Thomas Aquinas, which he observes to be even more illegible than his own. "I cannot even write properly myself, so that when I have finished a scrawl I had rather rewrite it than give myself the trouble of deciphering it." He makes friends with Anthony Bacon, a brother of the great Francis, and embarks upon a correspondence with him. His zest for life is insatiable. He indulges the fancy of being given the full citizenship of Rome. To be a Roman citizen! One can understand how of all others he would covet that distinction. He pursues his purpose "with all his five natural senses" and is accorded the honour. He goes about glancing now at this damsel, now

39

at that, never failing to allow due credit for beauty and charm.

But, of course, it is at home, in his serene and hospitable château of St Michel de Montaigne, that we are able to envisage him best. Here, within those cool, stone-flagged courtyards, the gates of which stood ever open to welcome king or beggar, " having no other guard than my porter, no other sentinel than the stars," his extraordinary personality " virgin from all law-suits " and " harbouring but a perplexed and uncertain knowledge about his money," found full scope for placid, unhampered development. Alternately, to and fro across the neighbouring country-side, the warring factions passed, devastating all that came in their way. But it would seem that both Catholic and Huguenot felt a strange reluctance to trouble the residence of the old, indulgent, philosophic opportunist, who, as he himself declares, would be as ready, at a pinch, to carry a taper " before the Dragon as before St George." Decade followed decade, and still the château of Montaigne remained intact on its green eminence, a symbol of civilised humanism and happy tolerance amid a crazed and distracted world.

In the famous room of his tower, surrounded by a library of over a thousand folios, Montaigne passed his days in peace, disturbed only by the reverberating echoes of the great bell above him as it was rung morning and evening for the Ave Marias to be held in the castle-chapel below. Here it was that the stout, good-natured, weather-beaten philosopher, crossing himself, as he tells us, whenever he yawned, composed his essays, played with his cat, or interviewed that honest lad that he had to his tailor, "whom I never knew guilty of one truth," or ate his bread without salt, or drank the wine "that they mix in the buttery two or three hours before 'tis brought in," and even then, old hedonist that he was, "not willingly out of common glass, but in those that are clear and transparent."

We are made to see the passing of his easy, indolent days almost as clearly as if we ourselves had shared with Henry of Navarre the privilege of being his guest. Sometimes, when the mood was upon him, he would go down into the great hall and play cards with his wife and daughter, or take a stroll in his secluded orchard. Then, again, with whimsical, incredulous eye, he would stand watching his long-suffering lady busying herself with her aromatic simples and medicinal herbs, or the inexpedient ways of the governess with his daughter Léonore.

Tired of this, he would go riding abroad over his lands, and although, as he confesses, he had " no manner of complacency for husbandry," he would while away his time talking to this or that familiar rustic, for he always, as he tells us, " had an inclination towards the meaner sort of people." Wherever he went there beat under his doublet a spleen-less and generous heart, a heart unexpectedly tender, as, for instance, when he assures us he could with difficulty watch a chicken being killed or hear the cries of a hare in her agony when the dogs had got her. Always simply enough dressed in black and white " in imitation of my father," he would return from such homely excursions to the perusal of his Plutarch, or even to the reading of Cicero, though he remarks that an hour with this latter formal stylist " was a great deal for him."

Little enough is known of his wife, the Lady Françoise de la Chassaigne. It

42

is apparent that Montaigne's attitude towards her was one of indulgent tolerance not unmingled with contempt.

" Feminine policy has a mysterious course and we must e'en let them go on their own way.

" There is a natural feud, a fray, between us and women ; the closest agreement that we have with them is more or less turbulent and stormy.

" I see, and I am vexed to see, in several families I know, Monsieur about dinner-time comes home all jaded and ruffled about his affairs when Madame is still pouncing and tricking up herself, forsooth, in her closet. This is for queens to do, and that's a question too ; 'tis ridiculous and unjust that the laziness of our wives should be maintained with our sweat and labour.

" The pains of child-bearing, said by the physicians and by God himself to be very great, *and which our women keep such a clutter about*—there are whole nations that make nothing of them.

" I for my part went ever the plain way to work.

" I love to lie hard and alone, yea, even without my wife, as kings do.

43

"And as great a libertine as I am taken to be, I have in truth more strictly observed the laws of marriage than I either promised or expected.

"Who for seeing me one while cold and presently very fond towards my wife, believes the one or the other to be counterfeited is an ass."

There have been many who have had it in them to dispute Montaigne's claim to be considered as a serious philosopher. They are mistaken. If wisdom is philosophy, what a rich store of it is contained in these quaint, closely written pages. It is a Shakespearean wisdom, a wisdom that is simple and that springs as naturally from the pasture-lands and parks of Warwickshire as from the vineyards of Guyenne. When we loiter near some place full of suggestions of age-long human usages— a graveyard perhaps, or a sheep-shearing barton, or a blacksmith's forge when horse-shoeing is in progress—and overhear some pithy comment that seems to have the very sap of life in it, we are listening to the voice of Montaigne. John Cowper Powys, in his *Suspended Judgments*, has after his poetic manner expressed this most excellently :

44

" The wisdom of Montaigne is the wisdom of lazy noons in spacious corn-fields, of dewy mornings in misty lanes and moss-grown paths; of dreamy shadows in deep grass when the apple boughs hang heavily earthward, and long nights of autumn rain have left amber-coloured pools in the hollow places of the trees and in the mud trodden by the cattle. . . . It is the wisdom of the earth itself; shrewd, friendly, full of unaccountable instincts; obstinate and capricious, given up to irrational and inexplicable super-stitions, sluggish, suspicious, cautious, hostile to theory, enamoured of incon-sistencies, humorously critical of all ideals, realistic, empirical, wayward."

Montaigne himself affirmed that there should be " nothing more airy, more gay, more frolic, and I had like to have said more wanton, than philosophy "; and cer-tainly if one takes some of his utterances at random one is astounded at the deep, lætificant sagacity which they reveal. In the mean, famished period in which we live, wherein ill-bred industrial commer-cialism masquerades as civilised life, how consoling, how infinitely restorative they are, as it were like great dripping combs

45

of golden honey gathered from I know not what distant blossoms !

" Man (in good earnest) is a marvellous, vain, fickle, and unstable subject, and one on whom it is very hard to form a certain and uniform judgment.

" I would always have a man to be doing . . . and then let death take me planting my cabbages, indifferent to him and still less of my garden's not being finished.

" They begin to teach us to live when we have almost done living. A hundred students have gotten the pox before they have come to read Aristotle's lecture on temperance.

" There is indeed a certain low and moderate sort of poetry, that a man may well enough judge by certain rules of art; but the true supreme and divine poetry is above all rules and reason . . . it does not exercise but ravishes and overwhelms our judgments.

" All whimsies as are in use amongst us deserve at least a hearing.

" A young man should often plunge even into excesses, otherwise the least vice will ruin him, and he also is apt to become tiresome and *inconvenient in conversation*.

46

"Women are not in the wrong when they refuse the rules of life obtaining in the world; it is the man who made these laws without them.

"The for and the against are both possible.

"I am a man and nothing human is alien to me."

So taken was Montaigne himself with the last two sentences that he caused them to be engraved upon the ceiling of his tower. It seems he was often in doubt concerning the intrinsic value of his writings, though he never allowed such misgivings to ruffle his accustomed equanimity. "I do not, nevertheless, always believe myself; I often hazard sallies of mine own wit, wherein I very much suspect myself and shake my ears; but I let them go at a venture." After all, what did it matter? "If I should have a long life my memory is so bad that I believe I shall forget my own name. So greatly do I excel in forgetfulness that even my writings are forgotten. The public dealeth me blows about them, and I do not feel them." Should his papers eventually be used as wrappers he makes little of it: "I shall at least keep

47

some pats of butter from melting in the market."

Montaigne died at his château in his sixtieth year. The grapes that covered so closely those sun-drenched, hand-cultivated slopes had already been harvested, and already the trees that held with so firm a root to the opulent soil of his broad acres were changing colour. " In the last piece between death and you there is no pretending; you must speak French."

On 13th September 1592 Michel de Montaigne, having distributed certain legacies to his servants, summoned his parish priest to his bedside, and there in his curious room, with the swallows already gathering on the leaden gutters outside, he heard Mass said for the last time, in the company of certain of his neighbours. With due solemnity the Blessed Sacrament was elevated, and at the very moment that this good heretical Catholic and Catholic heretic (unmindful for once of his nine learned virgins) was raising his arms in seemly devotion toward the sacred morsel which in its essence—*que sçais-je*—might, or might not, contain a subtle and crafty secret, he fell back dead.

CHRISTOPHER MARLOWE

CHRISTOPHER MARLOWE

THOUGH we have in our possession such scanty records of his life, few names in English literature stir us to more romantic speculations than does that of Christopher Marlowe. " A boy in years, a man in genius, a God in ambition," his wild and attractive personality flashes across the spacious firmament of the Elizabethan era with all the startling and sudden beauty of a falling star. From the first a certain suggestion of impending disaster seems to have surrounded the brief years of his wayward life. It was as though the winds that blew upon him from the outer spaces were electric and sultry ; as though in truth it might have been foreknown that his passage to immortality would be as fatal as it was swift. The very subjects which he selected for his plays were significant : the story of the blasphemous Scythian King ; the story of the reckless scholar of Wertenberg ; the story of the unhappy English monarch so disastrously susceptible to the physical beauty of his friends.

Born but a few months before William Shakespeare, Marlowe had none of the greater poet's attitude of homely, sagacious indulgence. Again and again in Marlowe's work one comes upon traces of an intellectual impatience, an engaging temper of youthful bravado, which drew him irresistibly towards those aspects of life which were likely to shock conventional susceptibilities.

In Marlowe's brilliant person the Italian Renaissance had found at last the very incarnation of its own aweless and resplendent spirit, actually abroad, so to speak, in the rambling, grimy, gibbous streets of old London. It is, therefore, no great wonder that the name of Kit Marlowe should have been a rallying cry to generations of golden youths in their careless revolt against the restrictions of adult prudence.

It is to be regretted that there is nothing extant to give us the slightest hint of the kind of physical grace which without doubt helped much to endear this son of a Canterbury cobbler to men like Sir Walter Raleigh and Sir Thomas Walsingham. Perhaps it was the very humbleness of his origin, with its abstinence and austerity of living, which set the "pure elemental wit" of Kit Marlowe so uncompromisingly towards those experiences from which his eager senses might be expected to extract their most vivid satisfactions. We are, at any rate, justified in surmising that the low, darkened, oak-panelled room in the left-hand corner of the old Court of Corpus was privy to many a wild, imaginative flight while it was occupied by that "rare-witted" scholar, who, although scarce of man's estate, was already yearning for a thousand fantastical adventures. Small marvel that even to this day, as the present writer can testify, the young men who are privileged to frequent those historic precincts cherish the memory of the famous poet who, three or more centuries ago, passed in riotous gaiety from stairway to stairway across the egg-shaped cobblestones which still pave the more secluded quadrangle of the oldest college in Cambridge.

It has been suggested that Marlowe was influenced by the unfortunate Kett, who, himself a Corpus man, was burned for heresy in 1589. If this was indeed the case, it is very certain that the young disciple soon outdid the somewhat mild

53

mysticism of his master. For it is quite as clear from the internal evidence of his writings as from the reports, legends and ballads that are connected with his name that Marlowe, in his search " for brave translunary things," was completely " lord of his desires," acknowledging neither check nor boundary. Indeed, with that misguided wilfulness which so often seems to be associated with intelligence, it would appear that he felt no compunction whatever in discounting with the most distressing levity the great truths of the Christian religion !

It has been assumed that his Cambridge degree was intended to give him entrance to the Church. If this was so, the plan sadly miscarried. After leaving the university we find him adrift in London, writing plays and living the free, delightful life of an artist, the friend of Peele and Greene, poets from whom he differed, if we are to believe that energetic and discriminating prose writer, Algernon Charles Swinburne, " not in degree, but in kind; not as an eagle differs from wrens or titmice, but as an eagle differs from frogs or tadpoles."

His first play won for him immediate recognition, and during the following

54

years until his death he was occupied with literary work. It is evident that Shakespeare himself fell under the spell of his genius, not only appreciating the value of his " mighty line," but seeking his assistance in several of his own plays. May we not also perhaps be permitted to read into the famous couplet of *As You Like It*, in which Shakespeare apostrophises his dead companion, a certain wistful tenderness?

What an exciting element the reckless, amorous youth must have brought to that noble company of poets who, when the playhouses were closed at last, gathered about the sea-coal fire of the Mermaid Tavern!

" What things have we seen
Done at the Mermaid! heard words that have been
So nimble, and so full of subtle flame
As if that every one from whence they came
Had meant to put his whole wit in a jest,
And had resolved to live a fool the rest
Of his dull life."

There has been an attempt lately, amongst certain tender-minded people, to bring the memory of Kit Marlowe more into line with the estimable standards of middle-class life. In this undertaking none has shown more enthusiasm and ingenuity than his late biographer, Mr Ingram, whose name, by a coincidence, is identical with one often given as that of Marlowe's murderer. The most cursory reading of Marlowe should be sufficient to show how hard a task Mr Ingram had before him. After a few pages have been turned it becomes clear that the tradition which has hung about the scapegrace playwright for three hundred years was " no pleasant burlesque of mine ancients." For all its " midsummer madness," no play could be more heathen in its conception and treatment than *Tamburlaine*.

" Come, let us march against the powers
      of Heaven
And set black streamers in the firmament
To signify the slaughter of the Gods.
  .   .   .   .   .
Come, let us charge our spears and pierce
      the breast
Whose shoulders bear the axis of the
      world."

The Tragical History of Dr Faustus also is packed with the equivocal writing of

56

one " swollen with cunning, of a self-conceit." Could the passionate idolatry of a pagan in frenzied ecstasy at the mere sight of the sweet flesh of a mortal find better expression than in his famous address to Helen of Troy?

Again and again certain lines emerge in his prologues, plays and poems which have upon them the very shape and colour of his rash, unregenerate temperament.

" For that fine madness still he did retain
Which rightly shall possess a poet's brain."

That his genius "at least delighted to dally with interdicted subjects " is made evident in a certain famous speech in his *Edward II.*, and also in numerous passages of *Hero and Leander*. Incidentally, in that last wonderful poem, with what consummate art he brings before our minds the peculiar desolate loneliness of " some old seaside knightly hall " built on the very cliff's edge !

" Far from the town, where all is whist
    and still,
Save that the sea, playing on yellow sand,
Sends forth a rattling murmur to the
    land."

57

His attitude to all wanton pleasure is also sufficiently clear in such lines as :

" The richest corn dies, if it be not reapt ;
Beauty alone is lost, too warily kept."

" O, that ten thousand nights were put in one
That we might sleep seven years together afore we wake ! "

" Tut, she were fitter for a tale of love
Than to be tired out with orisons :
And better would she far become a bed
Embraced in a friendly lover's arms
Than rise at midnight to a solemn Mass."

The following lines, one fears, must always be painful reading for critics of Mr Ingram's kind :

" I count religion but a childish toy
And hold there is no sin but ignorance."

" Then, if there be a Christ, as Christians say
But in their deeds deny him for the Christ."

" Becomes it Jews to be so credulous ? "

" The Christians—ringing with joy their superstitious bells."

If further evidence be required in support of the older tradition concerning Marlowe's irreligion, we must turn to the informer's writing which led the authorities to record in their books in May 1593 the four sinister words, " *He is lay'd for.*" The incriminating paper is preserved in the British Museum. " A Note contayninge the opinion of one Christopher Marlye, concernynge his damnable opinions and judgment of relygion and scorne of God's worde."

The original text is so outrageous that it has never been published in its entirety. It may be well, however, to remind the reader of certain of its less scurrilous passages :

" He *affirmeth* that Moyses was but a Juggler and that one Heriots being Sir Walter Raleigh's man can do more than hee.

" That it was ane easye matter for Moyses, beinge brought up in all the artes of the Egiptians, to abuse the Jewes, being a rude and grosse people.

" That all the appostells wer fishermen and base fellows neither of witt nor worth, that Pawle only had witt, that he was a timerous fellow in biddinge men to be subject to magistrates against his conscience.

"That if he [Kit Marlowe] wer put to write a new religion, he wolde undertake both a more excellent and more admirable methode, and that all the new testament is filthily written.

". . . that all protestants ar hipocriticall Asses."

Before Henry Maunder could execute the warrant, which had been put into his hands for Christopher Marlowe's arrest, the young poet was dead and buried in the old churchyard of St Nicholas Deptford. His end overtook him in the tavern of that village on 1st June 1593. The story of it is derived from various sources. It is reported that he was stabbed in the eye by "a bawdy serving-man, a rival of his lewd love . . . and in such sort that, notwithstanding all the means of surgery that could be brought, he shortly after died of his wound." It is further reported that he "cursed and blasphemed to his last gasp, and together with his breath an oath flew out of his mouth."

The unhappy event was duly put on record in the church register, where it may be read to-day: "Christopher Marlow, slain by ffrancis Archer (Ffrezer?) the 1st of June, 1593."

"So our tragical poet, Marlow, for his Epicurisms and Atheisme had a tragical death," mildly commented a contemporary; while Thomas Beard, the Puritan, with that ignorant obtuseness which so often characterises men of his kind in their relations with the finer æsthetic values of life, had the full hardihood to exclaim with malevolent glee: "See what a hooke the Lord put in the nostrils of this barking dogge!"

TOM CORYAT

TOM CORYAT

THE village of Odcombe, in the county of Somerset, is situated on the edge of a green, windswept hill overlooking Sedgemoor and the Vale of Avalon.

In former times the coach road from London to Exeter ran through the village, and there still may be seen an old milestone with the words " 107 miles to Hyde Park Corner " plainly discernible on its lichen-covered surface.

Was it perhaps, one wonders, the motley, unending stream of old-world traffic along this very thoroughfare, with its pack-horses and wain-oxen, that first fired the imagination of Tom Coryat with a desire for foreign travel?

Tom Coryat, " that great lunatique," as John Donne called him, was the son of George Coryat, the Elizabethan incumbent of Odcombe. He was born in 1577 and died in 1617. In the year 1608 he set out for Venice, travelling for the most part on foot, and a few years later published an account of his wayfaring in a volume which he quaintly entitled, *Coryat's crudities gobbled up in five months' travels: newly digested in the hungry air of Odcombe, in the county of Somerset.*

And what a born traveller he was, this glib Elizabethan who, upon his safe return, indulged the strange whimsey of hanging up his shoes in his father's church, where they remained on view for nearly two centuries.

The journal is written in so idiosyncratic and native a manner that all that he sees or experiences is brought home to the mind of the reader with extraordinary vividness.

Indeed, as we turn the faded pages we seem won to a strange intimacy with this inquisitive, bearded and fantastical figure, who, with clout on back and hedge stick in hand, made his way three hundred years ago along the dusty summer roads of Europe.

His curiosity was insatiable.

As he trudged stoutly forward from village to village nothing escaped his notice.

Now he is peering over the hedges " at the marvellous store of goodly oxen whereof almost all were dunne "; now he is observing " the abundance of little hip-frogges " ; now, loitering in a village street to see " a miscreant being beaten by a constable who was so stout a fellow that, though he received many a bitter lash, he did not a jot relent at it."

True countryman that he was, he must be for ever comparing what he saw with the sights and customs of his own home.

And it must not be forgotten that the background of Coryat's life was the England of Shakespeare's time, the England of stately manor-houses, of park and pasture-lands, of pleasant glebes and goose-greens, with men planting mulberry-trees here and oak-trees there, and eating of " shepherd's homely curds " and drinking of sack out of great leather flagons.

At Moulis, Coryat remarks " that the oxen and kine are coupled together with yokes and not loose as our oxen and kine are sold at fairs and markets in England."

At Pon de Beauvoisin " the barley was almost ripe to be cut, whereas in England they seldom cut the harvest before the beginning of August, which is almost three months later."

A plot of arable land near Basle " contayneth at least six times as much

67

in compasse (according to my estimation) than the great corn field of that famous manor of Martock in Somerset."

The precipices in Switzerland he finds to be "as deepe as Paul's Tower in London is high."

He cannot eat off a Swiss trencher without declaring it to be "as large in compasse as a cheese in my county of Somersetshire that will cost a shilling."

He cannot walk across the Piazza in Venice but he must needs wish to have it flagged with Ham Hill stone, as is the magnificent house of Sir Edward Phelips at Montacute.

Indeed he cannot even hear that a certain Italian poet called Jacobus Sannazarius had been awarded a hundred crowns but he wishes "his poetical friend, Mr Benjamin Jonson, were so well rewarded, seeing that he hath made as good verses (in my opinion) as those of Sannazarius."

And what an epicure the feather-heeled rascal is!

Like many another honest traveller, who is prepared to sit all day long on a settle in the sun under a swinging sign, he has a fine relish for a cup of good liquor.

In Milan he tells us he was actually sick " with a great distemperature in my body by drinking the sweet wines of Piemont," and at Heidelberg he went near to having a nasty fall from the gigantic tun of Rhenish wine upon which he had climbed.

But he is receptive in other ways, also.

He visits Livy's garden and it is not so much thoughts of the old Latin that occupy his attention as a " goodly apricock tree passing-well laden with fruits " which grew there.

And does not this convey the idea of a fine sensitiveness to the quality of a summer garden in June, " a great abundance of pleasant fruits and sundry walks and the sweetest grove for contemplation that ever I saw, being round about beset with divers delicate trees that at the springtime made a very fair show."

Certainly Tom Coryat had the power of assimilating and absorbing all that he saw. He carried home with him no vague impressions. He, so to speak, examined carefully every piece of iron, every cobble-stone, every worm-eaten beam of the cities that he visited, examined them till

he came to know these objects as well as
he knew the signpost between Odcombe
and Ilchester, the monk's dove-cot at
Montacute, or the stirrup-stone near the
old Turnpike house at Pye Corner.

Not content with observing the two
famous pillars in the piazza of St Mark's
at Venice, built, as he tells us, " by a very
cunning architect," he must stretch his
arms round them so as to ascertain their
exact measurements. In the same way he
was at pains to touch the " yron coffin
of St Luke . . . with some difficulty, for
it was so farre within the grate that I could
hardly conveigh the tops of my fingers to
it." He must himself " make a glasse at
Murano," himself taste the cool, refreshing water of the well in the courtyard of
the Doge's Palace, himself clamber to the
dusty timbered roof above the belfry of
the Campanile.

Perhaps it is this very faculty of his,
this faculty of taking possession, in an
almost physical way, of what he sees that
enables him in a few lines to convey to
the reader such an extraordinary sense of
reality. Little vignettes of foreign lands
are brought before us in a most vivacious
and lively manner, as though we ourselves

had but yesterday looked upon them. Take this for instance: " I saw but one horse in all Venice during the space of six weeks that I made my abode there, and that was a little bay nagge feeding in the churchyard at St John and Paul," and this, " I observed a great multitude of country clownes that came the Sunday morning to Mantua that I was there with strawen hats and feathers in them, and everyone that has his sithe and hooke in his hand ; belike they come to put themselves out to hire for harvest worke."

It is pretty to see how, like almost all Englishmen of his period, he cherishes a childish veneration for his well-loved home and " the mettle of its pastures."

He comes across a portrait of King James hung up in Venice among other European sovereigns, and because it is placed in the most important position he is " filled with content."

He looks over the French King's stables, where he saw " some fine and fair geldings and nagges, but neither in fineness of shape comparable to our King's horses, nor, as I take it, for swiftness."

When the aged Grecian Bishop makes " worthy mention of one Mr Samuel

Slade, a Dorsetshire man born," " it did tickle my heart with joy."

But even his enthusiasm for England weakens before the virgin city of the Adriatic. Never has Venice had a more ardent admirer.

He loitered there for nearly two months and many and strange are the things he tells of his visit.

Very seriously he takes upon himself to caution the reader against the boatman at the ferry near the Rialto, " the most vicious and licentious varlet about all the city. For if a stranger entereth into one of the gondolas and doth not presently tell him whither he will go, they will incontinently carry him of their own accord to a religious house forsooth ; where his plumes shall be well pulled before he cometh forth again."

As a matter of fact, one suspects that Coryat himself, in spite of his protestations to the contrary, was by no means averse to visiting such " religious houses."

Indeed, he writes at length on the subject of Venetian courtesans, stating amongst other things that the reason of their number being so great was that " the gentlemen of Venice held the opinion that if they should be rooted out the chastity of their wives would be the sooner assaulted and so consequently they should be capri-cornified (which of all indignities in the world the Venetian cannot patiently endure)."

His reference to the famous clock that still stands over the gateway leading from the piazza of St Mark's to the Rialto is piquant with all a countryman's wonder at civilised novelties.

He describes it first as " a very pretty conceit with the images of two wilde men by it, made in brasse, a witty device and very exactly done," and then goes on to relate how that " while he was in the Duke's Palace observing of matters," " A certain fellow that had the charge to look to the clocke was very busy about the bell to amend something in it that was amisse. In the meantime one of the wilde men that at the quarters of the howers doe use to strike the bell strooke the man on his head with his brazen hammer, giving him so violent a blow that therewith he fell down dead presently in the place and never spake more."

A favourite pastime with Coryat was to stand and listen to the mountebanks or " merry fellows." It amused his rustic humour " to hear them first extol their

73

wares up to the skies and set a price of
ten crowns and then descend so low that
they would take four gazels or something
less than a groat."

He was also impressed by the practice
common in Venice of burying laymen in a
Franciscan Friar's habit, especially if the
said layman had been a riotous and licentious
liver in his lifetime, by which means it was
hoped to cozen God at the day of judgment.

Fortified, doubtless, by the consoling
attitude of the Church of England with
regard to such matters, he observed with
no little confidence " that we in England
do hope to obtaine remission of our sinnes
through the mere merits of Christ and not
by wearing a Friar's frocke to which we
attribute no more virtue than to a bardo-
cullus, that is a shepherd's ragged and
weather-beaten cloake."

From first to last Coryat was no mean
champion of the Church of England, " as
by law established."

The Papists he looked upon with dis-
trust, the Turks with something more
than suspicion, and the Jews with out-
raged indignation.

He was at all times ready to engage
in nice theological disputes.

74

At a certain tavern in France he entered into such " a violent argumentation in defence of Christ " with a certain Turk that the fellow was feign " to fling out of my company."

In the Ghetto in Venice this same zeal nearly got him into trouble. After having attended a service in a synagogue, he " insinuated himself into conference " with a certain learned Jewish Rabbi, and did not hesitate to point out to the old man " how lamentable it was for a Christian to merely consider the damnable estate of miserable Jews." In answer to which the indignant Hebrew, to the utter amazement of the simple-minded and importunate traveller, began muttering in his beard " that he esteemed the Lord for a carpenter's son and a silly poor wretch that rode on an asse."

It is quite clear that the wonderful spell of Venice held Thomas Coryat completely in thrall. His stay there, he says, " was the sweetest time that ever I spent in my life."

He actually goes so far as to declare that he would not have forgone seeing it if he had been promised four of the richest manors of Somerset.

" While I live I will say that the sight

of Venice and her resplendent beauty hath by many degrees more contented my mind and satisfied my desire than the four Lordships could possibly have done." And we know on the word of Ben Jonson that for many years afterwards was the city Venice but mentioned in Coryat's presence " he would break doublet, crache elbow, and over flowe the roome with his murmur."

Very soon after the publication of his *Crudities* Tom Coryat started out on a new expedition.

This time he ventured into Asia, even getting as far as India, but alas! he never lived to return home; for somewhere in remote Persia he died.

It is reported that as he lay sick and faint with thirst he fancied he heard the sound of the word " sack," that most consoling and liberal drink that he had on so many occasions quaffed in the homely ale-houses of the West Country.

" Sack! sack! Is there such a thing as sack? I pray you give me some sack," he kept crying, to the mystified strangers about him, and these were the last words ever spoken by this adventurous and gallant gentleman of Odcombe, England.

SIR THOMAS
URQUHART

SIR THOMAS URQUHART

ALL romancical lovers of English literature are grateful to John Willcock for his excellent monograph on Sir Thomas Urquhart, the inimitable translator of Rabelais.

The volume published some twenty years ago makes it possible for us to arrive at a very fair conception of the honest knight whose mellow conceits have been, and will ever be, so much appreciated by a certain type of reader.

Less learned than Burton, less serious than Sir Thomas Browne, he holds a unique position among men of letters of the seventeenth century.

Not only was he the dandified thaumaturge that looks out upon us from the famous etchings by George Glover, but also, be it said, no mean philosopher. For the most casual observation of his style reveals the fact that he had in his possession some enigmatic secret which enabled him to preserve an intellectual detachment most quaint and crazy, amid the prodigious banalities of the world.

Jerked to and fro, as he undoubtedly was, by destiny, one suspects that in every phase of the hazardous puppet-show the last laugh came from his own aristocratic lips.

Indeed, it is as if the familiar chess-board of Kings and Presbyters, of Castles and Knights, over which he moved was but the phantasmagoria of some roguish old-wives' tale.

When he is on his travels it is not the Princes of Italy or the Prelates of Spain that impress his strange humour, but the fact that he met a man in Venice " who believed he was sovereign of the whole Adriatic," and another in Madrid " who thought himself to be Julius Cæsar and therefore went constantly into the streets with a laurel crown on his head."

His debts, he confides to us, were enough to " appal the most undaunted spirits and kill a very Paphlogonian partridge that is said to have two hearts." And the Presbyters, whom he so hated, he does not hesitate to dub " cocklimatory wasps " or " evil eggs of evil crows " whose " wretched peevishness " should debar them from all honest conversation.

Every one of his writings and utterances

has the same disconcerting turn or twist, so that at the last the bewildered readers of his works are completely " metagrabolised " and can tell no better than one of his own " Chitterlings " whether the worthy knight is to be taken seriously or not.

How was it that Sir Thomas Urquhart managed to reach so happy a state of detachment in a world which other mortals are wont to take with such ponderous gravity ?

Was it, one wonders, from observing the eccentric wisdom of his great-uncle, John Urquhart of Craigfintray, who was so renowned " for his deep reach of natural wit and dexterity in acquiring possessions with *all men's applause* " or from listening, perhaps, to the shrewd words of some Cullicudden midwife who had taken stock of her life's occupation with a " blinkard mind " and come to her own dour conclusions ?

Sir Thomas was born in 1611. His home was the old embattled Castle of Cromartie, whose dark-stained turrets rose no less than one hundred and sixty feet above the village. It was in his library there that this Scottish Montaigne on his return from his travels occupied himself with such matters " as the reasons for the variety of colours, and the squaring of a circle."

He himself gives us some vivid glimpses of his life during those far-off days.

While his friends would go tramping over the frozen marshes, he of a winter's afternoon would remain closeted in the castle, losing himself in those curious investigations which with a scholar's partiality he declares to be " worth more than six hundred thousand moor-fowl."

How well we can see his fanciful laced figure in that great tapestried room, sitting goose-quill in hand, close up against the generous fireplace " within the chimney of which two threshers could ply their flails " !

How well we can see him, Cotgrave's dictionary shut at last, stepping across to the tall diamond-paned window to peer with quizzical interest at the familiar constellations whose dim starlight (before ever Cor Caroli had appeared in the heavens) shone down upon the grey stone tiles of the castle roof, and upon the silent cobble street below, and upon the restless darkness of the sea !

82

This happy and undistracted period of Sir Thomas' life soon, however, came to an end. The fortunes of the house of Urquhart experienced evil days. For the old man his father, the courteous Grangousier of Cromartie, in that he considered it " derogatory to the nobility of his house to look too closely into his own purse," fell into debt.

It was in vain that his two sons, Thomas and Alexander, endeavoured to right the tottering fortunes of the castle. In spite of the fact that their zeal actually led them on one occasion to imprison the spendthrift old gentleman from a Monday to a Friday " within an upper chalmer called the inner Dortour " things continued to go from bad to worse.

The very civil war, we are told, was welcomed by the distressed family, bringing as it did relief from " hornings " and "apprisings " and " huddling up the terms of Whitsuntide and Martinmas which in Scotland are for the payment of debts."

In 1641, having taken sides against the Presbyters, Thomas went to England, where in one of the galleries of Whitehall he received a knighthood from King Charles.

His father died in the following year, bequeathing to him " in worldly goods twelve or thirteen thousand pounds sterling of debt, five brethren all men and two sisters almost marriageable."

From this time Sir Thomas suffered nothing but torments at the hands of creditors who seemed to derive a peculiarly malignant satisfaction from aggravating their whimsical bankrupt. Robert Lesly of Findrassie actually had audacity enough to take possession of one of his outlying farms " to which," as the indignant Lord of the Manor assures us, " he had no more right than to the town of Jericho mentioned in the scriptures." Others, and these Sir Thomas seems especially to have resented, would " pluck him away from his studies by their importunity," even going so far as to lay hold on his beloved books.

Always a stout Royalist, he marched with Prince Charles into England and fought at the battle of Worcester. It was here that the greatest of all calamities overtook him, for not only were the King's troops routed and himself taken prisoner, but his much-cherished manuscripts, the very quintessence of his work in the

84

library of Cromartie Castle, were lost. He had left them packed in "three portmantles" in the house of Master Spilsbury, "a very honest man who hath an exceeding good woman to his wife," but in the confusion that succeeded the battle they fell into the hands of two of Cromwell's soldiers, "exquisite snaps or clean shavers," who scattered them through the streets of the town so that certain "piemakers" seizing upon them put them to the scurvy use of wrapping up "figs, dates, almonds, and caraway." One or two pages however (the value of which in Sir Thomas' opinion could hardly be over-estimated) were picked up by one Master Broughton, a drizzling rain having lodged them in the mud. And this intelligent Roundhead, immediately recognising their worth, made, as we are informed, "all inquiry he could for trial whether there were any more such quinternions or no." By such means enough were eventually recovered to serve as a foundation for the *Jewel picked up in the kennels of Worcester Streets the day after the fight and six before the autumnal Equinox anno* 1651—a prose work which was put into print a few years later.

85

It now fell to the lot of Sir Thomas Urquhart to spend several years as a state prisoner, first in the Tower of London, afterwards at Windsor. That Cromwell would continue to keep him behind stone walls if once he came to realise the choice quality of his erudite and ingenious spirit was inconceivable to Sir Thomas: so without more to-do he set about to prove to the preoccupied Protector, by means of his pen, the inestimable value to the Commonwealth of such an author.

It would be a difficult undertaking to pass judgment upon these works. They might have been the result of Panurge's collaboration with Thaumast, the Englishman. In them buffoonery and wisdom stand so intermixed that whether they reach the height of super-subtle sagacity or the depths of fantastical folly remains still an open question.

In his *Peculiar Promptuary of Time* he gravely traces the pedigree of the Urquharts to Adam surnamed "Protoplast," indicating thereby how sorry a thing it would be for a family, spared for so many ages by God, to be brought to confusion in 1655 by Oliver Cromwell!

It cannot be denied that his antecedents

were remarkable. The first to settle in Scotland was one Nomostor, son-in-law to Alcibiades, who arrived at Cromartie or Portus Salutus in 389 B.C. Even in historic times it is quite clear that his progenitors displayed a potency of character such as would naturally separate them from the rest of the human race. We learn, for instance, that Thomas Urquhart, born in 1474, was surnamed Paterhemon " because he had of his wife Helen, daughter of my Lord Salton, five and twenty sons all men and eleven daughters all married women."

His *Trissotetras* or, as he calls it, " A most exquisite Table for resolving all manners of Triangles published for those that are mathematically affected," is obviously designed to relieve an abstruse science of much of its monotony by the simple method of giving to each lineal symbol a proper name.

A short quotation should be sufficient to enable the reader to appreciate his method : " The axiums of plane triangles are four Rulerst Eproso, Grediftal, and Bagredifl while Rulerst branches into Gradesso and Eraetul is under the directory of Uphechet," etc. The grammar and

87

syntax of his *Logopandecteision or Universal Language Contrived for the Utilitie of All Pregnant Spirits* were " a pescod on it ! " lost at Worcester. Enough however escaped the pie-makers of that city to give a receptive linguist a fair idea of its possibilities. The language was made up of four numbers, eleven genders, and one word for each several idea.

With pardonable complacence Sir Thomas himself points out its especial merits. " Every word," he says, " signifieth as well backward as forward and however you invert the letters, still shall you fall upon significant words whereby a wonderful facility is obtained in the making of anagrams."

Finally we come to the famous translation.

There must indeed have been a rooted congruity between the fanciful Cavalier and the old French monk, for in this work all the cherished conceits of Urquhart's crested imagination found ample encouragment and scope.

In Rabelais' massive and broad-mouthed chapters he could expand and burgeon to his heart's content ; there being room and space enough for his gravest drollery and his hugest planetary quip. Here at last there was nothing to prevent him heaping up his page with epithets and synonyms like so many pieces of chopped peat banked against the woodshed in the castle yard of Cromartie. Often he does not hesitate to enlarge upon the original, serving up from his unctuous literary kitchens a largess of words as quaint and original as any used by the master himself.

In the well-known passage of the animal noises that disturbed the peace of the philosopher Rabelais is content with nine, but seventy-nine are scarcely sufficient for Sir Thomas Urquhart! And as a matter of fact how ill we could spare such inventions as the "cheeping of mice," "coriating of storks," "snottering of monkies" and "nuzzing of camels"!

Unbroken indeed is the silence surrounding the latter years of the philosopher of Cromartie. It is known that he crossed over to the continent of Europe, but that is all.

Did he, the Urquhart "Parresiastes" or "Free of Speech," grow mute and inarticulate at the last? We cannot tell. Only once, and that in the legend of his death, do we hear of him again. For it is

89

reported that when news came to him of the Restoration and the delight of the counties of England at the return of the royal house they had been at such pains to evict, he fell into so great a fit of Gargantuan laughter that it cracked his heart, dispatching the queer spirit of this abstractor of quintessences forthwith into the presence of its Maker.

IZAAK WALTON

IZAAK WALTON

IT would seem that gently flowing waters in some strange way lend themselves to thoughts of a meditative and religious complexion. It is reported of Confucius that whenever he sat by the side of a river he would cry, so deeply would his mind be disturbed by philosophic contemplations engendered by the sight of a gliding stream. And there is about the writing of Izaak Walton just this quality of reflective piety. As has been well said by Professor Saintsbury, there hangs over the pages of *The Compleat Angler* a " singular and golden simplicity."

The book carries with it the very sights and sounds and scents of sweet river-side pastures, the very glimpses of their wide silver reaches, the very cries of their half-hidden water-fowl—of moor-hens, coots and dabchicks, the very aromatic smells of the overgrown water-flowers that cluster about their damp margins. *The Compleat Angler*, Charles Lamb declared, " would sweeten a man's temper at any time to

read it," and indeed its " smooth writing "
has had a most consoling influence upon
generations of human beings who, less
wise or less fortunate than its author, have
had for their life's occupation not the
" disporte of fysshyng," but " the diligence
of trades and noiseful gain."

A certain similarity has been observed
between *The Compleat Angler* and Bunyan's
Pilgrim's Progress, and truly it would seem,
as one remembers the two books, that
something of the same lovely sunlight that
lit up the green slopes of the delectable
mountains falls also upon those glorified
meadows of the Thames which used to
seem to the old angler " too pleasant to
be looked upon but on holy days." It is
extraordinary how Izaak Walton has managed to convey to his readers the intense
relish and enjoyment that he was wont to
experience on the occasions when he was
able to leave his little shop in Fleet Street
and go a-fishing. Never has the peaceful
radiance of green fields under a May-day
sun been more surely described. From
each artless sentence, from the very words
he uses, there is evoked the actual look
of the gleaming spring grass, the actual
smell of the cowslip-grown meadow-sod

under the soft influence of a "smoking shower."

All day long in our fancy those enchanted meads seem to be echoing with "the curious ditties of the little nimble musicians of the air," while at night-time, "when the very labourers sleep," the nightingale holds them spellbound with the ecstasy that she pours out from her "instrumental throat." All day long between the cool shadows and cheerful sunshine of those verdant fields it would seem that boys and girls are out gathering lady-smocks and culverkeys.

And it is not only the green fields, but the whole country-side, of that far-off time that is brought before our eyes, that opulent homely country-side of England that even to-day has scarcely changed its familiar aspect from when Chaucer's Franklin enjoyed the largess of its acres.

" Ful many a fat patrich hadde he in mewe
And many a breem and many a luce in
    stew."

We ourselves actually see the grey park walls, the gnarled oak-trees, the graceful beeches ; we ourselves actually walk along the king's highway to Tottenham Cross under the cool shadow of a high honey-suckle hedge, with the golden disks of dandelions wide open in the ditch-grass, and our boots floury white with the first thin dust of early spring. We ourselves enter that "honest ale-house" and see with our own eyes the sweet marjoram, the sprigs of rosemary, the green aromatic parsley on the cleanly kitchen table, delicious friendly simples, awaiting the dressing of that trout whose belly when taken "was part yellow as a marigold and part white as a lily." We ourselves sit in the raftered guest-room and read one or other of the twenty ballads that are stuck about its walls, and later, when darkness has fallen and over the thatched roof and over the dreaming shire the stars of eternal space shine down, take our rest between those sheets that "smell of lavender" and are as white as the milk drawn by modest Maudlin from the udder of her red dairy cow.

There is in the writings of Izaak Walton a quality so devout, so charged with a simple unadorned beauty that it can only be described as "apostolic," and indeed one might almost fancy that certain of its more inspired passages were taken directly from the Scriptures, might have actually been written by one of the evangelists had chance led his holy steps to the flowering primrose banks of a river in England. "We anglers," Walton writes, "seldom take the name of God into our mouth, but it is either to praise him or to pray to him"; and again: "Let the blessing of St Peter be upon all that are lovers of virtue and dare trust in providence and be quiet and go a'fishing."

What a winning insight we get into the good old man's temperament and disposition as we read his book. Like George Herbert and like Sir Thomas Browne, he represents in his character that unassuming devoutness, that humane sanctity, liberal but at the same time catholic, that has appeared from time to time amongst the sons of the Church of England. And what a rooted affection he cherished for that decorous island religion! In his will, written on his ninetieth birthday, he boldly declares his attitude: "I take it at least to be convenient to declare my belief to be, in all parts of faith as the Church of England now professeth . . . I give to Dr Hawkins, Dr Donne's sermons which I have heard preacht and read with such

content." Again he refers to Dr Nowel,
Dean of St Paul's, as the man who " made
that good, plain, unperplexed catechism
which is printed with our good old service
book."

Always a stout Royalist, he had no love
for Puritans or doctrinal controversialists,
and constantly deplores the fact that " the
common people in this nation think they
are not wise unless they busy themselves
about what they understand not, and
especially about religion." He himself
put his own theological erudition to the
good purpose of justifying his favourite
pastime, pointing out with considerable
pertinence " that God is said to have
spoken to a fish, but never to a beast." In
his more secular researches his inquiring
and observing wit made record of some
extremely curious facts, facts that even he
confesses would appear to be as incredible
as the " resurrection of an atheist," but
which, for all that, he declares have their
place, " he whose name is Wonderful only
knows how " in the obscure ordering of
the laws of nature. There is, he asserts,
" a certain river that turns sheep's wool
to vermilion colour if they drink of it,"
and he also tells us that " the stones of

98

otters are good against the falling sickness,"
that "fish can smell an hundred yards
away," that "hares change sexes every
year," that "carp come to the surface at
the ringing of bells," that "smelt smell
like violets," and that eels "are bred of a
particular dew falling in the month of
May or June on the banks of some particular ponds or rivers apted by nature
for that end." Of the means by which
pike are brought into this world he is less
certain, at first declaring with significant
reticence that "some are bred by genera-
tion and some not" and then later suggest-
ing that they, in some mysterious way,
derive their life from pickerel weed. However, this initial uncertainty about the life's
history of these "tyrants of the water,"
as he calls them, by no means deters him
from further investigations. His "nice
curiosity" even explores the emotional
prejudices of this particular fresh-water
fish, for he does not hesitate to assure us
that "there has always existed between
pike and certain frogs a great antipathy."
Frogs, he declares, will make hard shift
to overreach pond pike "beyond common
belief." And he is at no loss to give
evidential support to his contention, for

he records how Bishop Thurzo, as he walked by one of his ponds, observed a frog, whose swollen cheeks expressed either malice or anger, to leap on to the head of a pike that was at hover near the surface of the water. They both sank together, and the good prelate, being inquisitive to discover the upshot of the strange incident, called his gardener and had the pond dragged. The pike when recovered was found to be dead and with both its eyes clawed out. The Bishop expressed no little surprise at such an issue, but the gardener, who doubtless had had more opportunity of studying the hidden ways of nature, exhorted the reverend dignitary to " forebear wondering," saying that " *he was certain that pikes were often served so.*"

Izaak Walton also affirms that he was told " by a person of honour now long in Worcester " that so cunning is the strategy of these irascible roguish frogs " that collars of tadpoles are often to be found hung like chains about the necks of pike to kill them." In this case, however, even Izaak Walton is unsure as to the immediate motive prompting the subtle and deadly proceeding. For he concludes his narration by saying, "*whether it be done for meat or malice must be to me a question.*"

If frogs had the best of it in their relations with pike, it was a far different matter when they fell into the hands of the old fisherman himself. In his directions for using frogs as bait he writes: "Put your hook—I mean the awning wire—through his mouth and out of his gills and with a fine needle and silk sew the upper part of his leg with only one stitch to the awning wire of your hook—and in so doing, use him as though you loved him; that is, harm him as little as you may possibly that he may live longer."

After reading such a passage, one can hardly wonder that Lord Byron was provoked to write:

" And angling too, that solitary vice . . .
Whatever Izaak Walton sings or says,
The quaint old coxcombe, in his gullet
Should have a hook and a small trout to
    pull it."

But Byron was not Izaak Walton's only critic. Richard Franck, a Cromwellian trooper, tells us that once at Stafford he faced the old man with his own writing, " urging his own argument upon him that pickerel weed of itself breeds pickerel (pike) and with such directness that the good honest man went huffed away."

What glimpses, with the very stamp of authenticity upon them, we get of the old angler from time to time. How well we can see him under " yonder sycamore " saying his grace before partaking of his radishes and powdered beef and bread! And what engaging thoughts doubtless he resolved in his sober mind as with fingers, silver-scaly from cleaning the weeds and grass from the gills and throat of a newly caught logger-headed chub, he sat there in the pleasant coolness munching at his brave breakfast! Now he would perhaps be weighing the possible advantage to be derived from his friend Oliver Henly's guarded secret for making the contents of his bait-box the more palatable by anointing it with one or two drops of the oil of ivy berries, now musing over the country saying that " perch will not bite till the mulberry-tree buds," now recalling that eels in a hard winter will unbed themselves and seek warmth in haystacks, and now brooding over the fact that tench are the physicians of fishes and carry in them a natural balsam.

The last piece of instruction he believed to have come through the Jews, a race of people who, he says, have carried down from past ages a vast amount of useful knowledge, and yet, so he declares—and surely in this case his vehemence cannot have been altogether dispassionate—" It is thought that they, or some spirit worse than they, first told us that lice swallowed alive were a certain cure for the yellow jaundice ! "

The old man died at Winchester on 15th December 1683, when all England lay under the iron grip of a severe and pinching frost. And as he lay dying under the shadow of that ancient and monumental edifice that holds beneath its cold flagstones the bones of William Rufus and a hundred other Englishmen of the old time, we are justified surely in believing that during " that last hour of his last day as his body melted and vapoured into spirit " his innocent and guileless soul was supremely conscious of the blessed assurance that it was about to enter, without dispute or hindrance, into the presence of that gentle Saviour of the world whose last taste of food on earth had been, as Izaak Walton himself reminds us, a fish.

JOHN BUNYAN

JOHN BUNYAN

NEVER was there a man who was more conscious of the drama of life than John Bunyan : never a man whose philosophy fell more pat upon the footprints of his earthly wayfaring. And the whole store of his simple meditations was derived directly from the Bible. The Bible and Bedfordshire — in those two words we have the sources from which he drew all his inspiration ; the grave, formidable sentences of the old Authorised Version working upon the imagination of a countryman whose days had for their background the familiar pastoral landscape of seventeenth-century England with its fields and elm-trees, its church steeples and turnpike ale-houses.

Every incident of his desperate spiritual struggles has for its setting some scene from the unsophisticated visible world that he knew so well. Indeed he could never rid his hungry, religion - haunted mind of the conception that the commonest pastimes of the old-world village life of

Elstow were actually taking place under the unclosing and awful eye of God! He could not go up into the belfry of the church tower to ring out the old year on a frosty winter's night but it was an action remarked upon by his conscience; he could not dance on the village green on a midsummer's evening without strange misgivings intruding themselves into his rustic head. The very puddles in the roads, the very settles by the way, the very adders in the grass, were associated in his mind with this or that religious experience. All the sights and sounds of nature brought with them their particular message—the " yawling, bawling cuckoo " in a wayside spinney, the swift-flying swallows circling about the old " Moot Hall," the " comely, ruddy dog-roses " in the dew-drenched field hedges, the glinting flint stones lying at the bottom of the River Ouse!

And yet it would be a mistake to bring an accusation of sentimentality against him. The very power of his style rests upon a certain quality of tough, racy realism. It is as infracturable and sinewy as a freshly grown willow sapling, and it has about it something of the robust aroma that belongs to the more sturdy kinds of wild

108

flowers such as yarrow and ground ivy. And yet how pathetic are the spiritual contests undergone by this strong, simple soul as they are revealed to us in his *Grace Abounding*. A single enigmatic text from Scripture would be sufficient to " dash and abash " his spirit so that it would fall into despair " like a bird shot from the top of a tree " and leave him to go " moping into the fields."

All day long as he worked at his pots and pans the terrible sound of hell fire was never out of his earshot, as it roared and raged " not so very far down under ground," below the cowslip-grown meadows that surrounded his cottage home. " Have ye forgot," he once cried to his awestruck congregation, " the close, the milk house, the stable, the barn, where God did visit you? " Then he would fall to wishing that " either there had been no Hell, or that I had been a Devil, supposing they were only tormentors." He counted man to be " the most doleful of all creatures." " Blessed," he thought, " were the conditions of the birds, beasts and fishes, for they had not a sinful nature. They were not to go to hell fire after death; they were not obnoxious to the wrath of God."

"Hell!" he somewhere exclaims, "who knows that is yet alive what the torments of Hell are? This word Hell gives a very dreadful sound." And again in describing the miserable state of those that die unrepentant: "They go as an ox to the slaughter and as a fool to the correction of the stocks; that is both senselessly and securely. O! but being come at the gates of Hell! O! but when they see those gates set open for them. Then they roar like lions, yell like dragons, howl like dogs . . . this however must not be till they have gone out of the sight and hearing of mortals whom they do leave behind them alive in the world."

In his cottage, by his own fireside, he would be continually thrown into an "exceeding maze" by some crafty and deceptive thought. "How can you tell but that the Turks have as good Scripture to prove their Mahomed Saviour as we have to prove our Jesus is?" Presently he would get up and leave his goodwife and go into the wood-shed behind his house to chop a stick, and lo! a new blasphemy would "bolt out of his heart." "How could he tell but that St Paul, being a subtle and cunning man, might have given himself up to deceive with strong delusions?" Or, worse still, might not the Holy Scriptures themselves be but a "fable and cunning story"? At last, after many years, by dint of much studying of the Bible, "wisdom did most sweetly visit my soul." And indeed every word that comes from him has upon it something of the tone of that ancient, sober-covered book, whose pages he had so constantly turned over with his hard-skinned, work-worn fingers.

But even after he had got possession of his soul and had become the evangelist of the district, he had his difficulties. At the time of his trial there were those who did not hesitate to liken him to Alexander the coppersmith and to suggest that he had far better leave the mending of souls and return to the soldering of his kettles and cauldrons. There were others who were not ashamed to make base insinuations against the moral character of the rough old tinker. "They reported," he tells us, "with the boldest confidence that he had his misses, his whores, his bastards, yea, and even two wives at once." No wonder he was roused to speak plain words! "My foes," he stoutly asserts, "have missed their mark in thus shooting at me. I am not the man. I wish they themselves be guiltless. If all the fornicators and adulterers in England were hanged up by the neck till they be dead, I, John Bunyan, the object of their envy, would still be alive and well." And if we may be allowed to take as truth what he himself tells us with regard to his attitude towards women, we can easily understand how particularly galling to him these calumnies were. " It is a rare thing to see me carry it pleasantly towards women . . . their company alone I cannot away with. I seldom so much as to touch a woman's hand : for I think these things are not so becoming to me." Indeed, when his friends protested that such salutations were but a piece of common civility, he urged them that it was " not a comely sight." And when they in return spoke of the " holy kiss," he asked them, pertinently enough, why they made baulks ; why they did salute the most handsome and let the ill-favoured go.

And yet John Bunyan was no small, sour-souled Puritan. There is evidence that his large, rude heart, being full of " a great softness and tenderness," was

capable of embracing within its ample
boundaries not only the person of his
beloved " King Jesus " and his little blind
daughter, but also the very rooks that
pecked for grain in the upturned furrows
of the Bedfordshire ploughed lands. " Oh,"
he exclaims in describing the sufferings
he underwent during his imprisonment,
" the thoughts of the hardships my poor
blind one might go under ! " And in his
sermons he was never weary of exhorting
his flock to " carry it lovingly towards
children rather than be churlish and severe
with them." " But oh ! how I now loved
those words that spake of a Christian's
calling ' Follow me,' ' Come after me,' and
oh ! thought I, that He would say so to me
too ! how gladly would I run after Him.
. . . Yea, I was now so taken with the
love and mercy of God that I remember
I could not tell how to contain till I got
home. I thought I could have spoken of
His love and have told of His mercy even
to the very crows that sat upon the ploughed
lands before me."

There are two stories that illustrate
very well the particular vein of shrewd
native humour that is characteristic of him.
It was his custom sometimes, when the

informers were more than usually active, to go to his meeting-places in disguise. On one such occasion, when he was driving along on a wagon dressed in a farm-labourer's smock, he was accosted by a constable who asked him if he knew " that devil Bunyan." " Know him ! " came back the answer, " you might well call him a devil if you knew him as well as I did once." Again, on being congratulated by some of his friends on the " sweet sermon " he had just preached, he replied : " Aye ! aye ! ye need not remind me of that ; for the Devil told me of it before I was out of the pulpit."

And what a racy understanding of life is revealed in his *Life and Death of Mr Badman*. It is an odd thing, but the style of this remarkable piece of writing reminds one more than anything else of Sir Thomas Urquhart's translation of Rabelais. Mr Badman, we learn, was most " arch in the sin of uncleanliness." " Cursing and swearing he made no more of than the telling of his fingers." " I can," he is made to say, " be religious and irreligious. . . . I can drink and wench and not be troubled for it. This I have attained with much study, care and pains." The poor,

114

meek woman, his wife, he would call " whore, bitch, and jade," and would constantly assure her " that it was well if she missed his fingers and heels." Eventually the rascal breaks his crown from a fall he took from his horse as he came home drunk from the tavern, thereby being in jeopardy of going pell-mell from " the pot to the grave." In his sickness he is seized with a most horrible fear of death, and his unhappy partner is suddenly transformed to " his dear wife, his Godly wife, his honest wife, his duck, his dear, and all." Sick-bed repentances, as Bunyan declares, are seldom of more value than " the howling of a dog," and upon Mr Badman's recovery his remorse counts for little, and his wife dies of a broken heart. Mr Badman now marries a woman of his own kidney, but soon comes to realise that he has been " catcht," to use Bunyan's sinister word. For his new lady, we are told, " could fit him with cursing and swearing, give him oath for oath and curse for curse." They would fight and fly at each other like cat and dog, and so they lived, she " with her rogues and he with his drabs, till they parted as poor as howlets."

The story certainly gives you an amaz-

ingly realistic glimpse of the ruder aspects
of life in England at the time of the
Restoration. Take for example the digres-
sion which tells of what John Bunyan
himself saw take place under the raftered
beams of the old tavern which " in Oliver's
days " stood a bow-shot from his door.
The old master of the place had a simple-
witted son called Ned, and it was a pastime of his to amuse his customers by
getting the lad to swear at him. We are
made to see the scene as if we ourselves
had been present, as if we ourselves had
been sitting amid the din and clatter of
those far-off days with the sunshine slanting down on the fields and thatched
cottage roofs outside. " I have heard
Ned, in his roguery, cursing his father
and his father laughing thereat, most
heartily and still provoking of Ned that
his mirth might be increased." And then
one day, all of a sudden, down fell the
father in a kind of fit which " the brave
fellows that did come to the tippling house
to fuddle and make merry " concluded
was caused by the Devil himself having
been summoned from Hell by the thought-
less words of the " innocent." Bunyan
assures us that they " were horrified to see

his flesh, as it was thought, gathered up in a heap about the bigness of half an egg, to the unutterable torture and affliction of the old man."

Sir Walter Scott and others have fostered the belief that John Bunyan came of gipsy forbears, but there is little evidence to support the supposition. His father is merely described as belonging to the "national religion." We know that at one time his illustrious son, believing that only Israelites were to be saved, made every effort to find some Hebrew blood in his descent, efforts which met with small encouragement from his father, the tinker, who, whatever his attitude may have been towards gipsies, had, so it appears, no ambition to be thought a Jew!

Bunyan himself somewhere writes: "I do confess myself one of the old-fashioned professors that wish to fear God and honour the King." Indeed, whenever he has occasion to allude to the sovereigns of England, it is always with respect. In one passage he even goes as far as to apply the epithet "noble" to Henry VIII. There is something touching about his references to the dissolute Charles as "his gracious Prince," and this after having suffered a

117

twelve-year imprisonment, " in that he had devilishly and perniciously abstained from coming to Church to hear Divine Service and was a common upholder of several unlawful meetings, to the great disturbance and distraction of the good subjects of the Kingdom."

His great work, *The Pilgrim's Progress*, was actually written in gaol, between the intervals of his making " long tagged laces." And what a fund of excellent matter the book contains !

" Thus I set pen to paper with delight
And quickly had my thoughts in black and
    white."

It was the one book beside *Robinson Crusoe* and *Don Quixote* that Dr Johnson would have had longer. It would seem a useless task to cull quotations from a volume which contains so many admirable passages. Where could we look for writing more vigorous and unaffectedly direct than this?—

" Now I saw in my dream that at the end of the valley lay blood, bones, ashes and the mangled bodies of men, even of pilgrims that had gone the way formerly ;

118

and while I was musing what should be the reason, I espied a little before me a cave where two great giants POPE and PAGAN dwelt in old times; by whose power and tyranny the men whose bones, blood, ashes, etc., lay there, were cruelly put to death. But by this place Christian went without much danger whereat I somewhat wondered: but I have since learnt that PAGAN has been dead many a day; and as for the other, though he be yet alive, he is, by reason of age, and also of the many shrewd brushes that he met with in his younger days, grown so crazy and stiff in his joints that he can now do little more than sit in his cave's mouth, grinning at pilgrims as they go by, and biting his nails because he cannot come at them."

Or would it be possible to find a passage of prose more chaste than the following:—

"Now as they were going along and talking they espied a boy feeding his father's sheep. The boy was in very mean clothes, but of a very fresh and well-favoured countenance; and as he sat by himself, he sang. Hark, said Mr Great-heart, to what the shepherd's boy saith. . . . So they hearkened, and he said—

119

" ' He that is down needs fear no fall ;
He that is low, no pride ;
He that is humble, ever shall
Have God to be his guide.'

" Then said the guide, Do you hear him ?
I will dare to say, that this boy lives a
merrier life, and wears more of that herb
called heart's-ease in his bosom, than he
that is clad in silk and velvet."

The Pilgrim's Progress was immediately
appreciated by the poor people of England. Innumerable editions were spread
broadcast and still there was a demand for
more. But this sudden renown made little
difference to the manner of John Bunyan's
life.

He died in his sixtieth year in the
house of his friend John Strudwick, a
grocer at the Sign of the Star, on Snow
Hill, Holborn, London. He died " like
a lamb, or, as men call it, like a chrisom
child, quietly and without fear." " Take
me, for I come to Thee ! " are reported
to be the last words he spoke. And surely
it is not impossible to believe that in the
inscrutable ordering of the Universe the
ardent faith of this simple, good man some-
how, somewhere, found its justification.

NICHOLAS CULPEPER

NICHOLAS CULPEPER

ON the shelves of old-fashioned libraries an inquisitive investigator will occasionally find himself confronted by the works of Nicholas Culpeper. Although the seventeenth-century herbalist's chief concern was with the hidden virtues contained in plants, his books have always held a distinct place among the curiosities of literature. He was born in 1616, the son of an English clergyman. Upon the outbreak of the Civil War he espoused the cause of Parliament, was wounded in the chest, and for the rest of his life settled down in the East End of London as an unofficial practitioner.

There is one especially curious incident recorded of Culpeper's youth. He had arranged, we, are told, to elope with a· young heiress, who, as she hurried to the trysting-place—" Mars and the envious planets intervening "—was struck dead by lightning. We cannot help fancying that it may very well have been this strange and untoward experience, beyond the bounds of reason, that was responsible for giving to Culpeper's mind that particular ironic twist that is so fascinating a characteristic of it.

A friend and brother astrologer informs us that he was in the habit of "mingling matters of levity with things of the most serious concernment and extremely please himself in so doing." Thus, in writing about his cure for melancholy, we find him ending his treatise in words that seem not altogether devoid of intellectual malice : "By this I mean not the simple complexion of melancholy, for without that none can live." Such, then, was the whimsical nature of the sad, droll, fantastical man, who for the space of nearly twenty years laboured, day in and day out, amongst the poorest inhabitants of Spitalfields, never refusing money or assistance to those who asked it of him, and never leaving a death-bed until his patient "had gotten out of life easily."

Naturally enough, Culpeper became extremely popular with the poor of London, some of them even going so far as to attribute his medicinal skill to magical power. It was with their support that he ultimately took upon himself to beard the official medical world by endeavouring to make accessible all the jealously guarded secrets of their trade. What till that time had been written only in Latin for the privileged few he set about to spread broadcast, in a series of tracts and booklets, amongst the drabs and footpads of Wapping Old Stairs. The degree of savage animosity that was roused by this bold proceeding may be gauged by the reception given to his *Pharmacopœia Londinensis* by the Royal Society of Apothecaries. " A work," declared this learned society, " done most filthily into English by one Nicholas Culpeper, who by two years of drunken labour hath gallimawfried the apothecaries' books into nonsense, mixing every receipt therein with some samples at least of rebellion and atheism."

Quite undaunted by this unrestrained outburst, their bizarre opponent promptly issued a second volume " Wherein Nic Culpeper brings, from under his velvet jacket, challenges against the Doctors of Physic and all the knick-knacks of astrology exposed for the first time to open sale." This compilation his enemies did not hesitate to declare had been written not only for the purpose of " bringing into

obloquy the famous societies of Apothecaries and Chyrurgeons," but also " to
supply his drunkenness and lechery with
a thirty-shilling reward."

Quite apart from the fascinating odd-
ness of the man's character, his works are
by no means without value, initiating, as
they do, the reader at first hand into that
quaint atmosphere of old wives' wisdom
by which the lives of our ancestors were
surrounded. Here, for example, are some
of the famous recipes presented " to the
courteous reader " by the sagacious old
leech of Red Lion Farm :

" *Marsh Mallows* : Bruised and well
boiled with milk and the milk drunk is a
gallant remedy for the gripings of the
belly [It was with this receipt he assures
us that he cured his own son.]—the
blessing of God be upon it ! He was
suffering from the plague of the guts and
I, here, to show my thankfulness to God,
do leave it to posterity.

" *Alder Tree* : The leaves put under bare
feet gauled with travelling are a great
refreshing to them. The said leaves also
gathered, when the morning dew is on
them, and brought into a chamber troubled
with fleas, will gather them there unto,

126

which being suddenly cast out will rid the chamber of these troublesome bed-fellows.

"*Barberry*: Mars owns this shrub and presents it to the use of my countrymen to purge their bodies of choler.

"*Sweet Bazil*: All authors are together by the ears about it. Myaldus reports that if laid to rot in horse dung it will breed venomous beasts, and Hilarius affirms, upon his own knowledge, that an acquaintance of his by the smelling of it had a scorpion bred in his brain. I myself am confident that the ointment of it is one of the best remedies of a scabby head that is.

"*The Vine*: A most gallant plant very sympathetical to the body of man."

A few remedies for specific weaknesses of the human race, both moral and physical, taken at random from Culpeper's book of Aphorisms, are not without interest for present-day readers:

"*Against drunkenness*: Eat six or seven bitter almonds every morning fasting: drink a draught of wormwood beer, also burn swallows in a crucible, feathers and all, and eat a little of the ashes of this in the morning.

"*Against the gout*: Take an owl, pull off

her feathers, pull out her guts. Salt her well for a week. Bring to mummy and mix with bear's grease is an excellent remedy, annointing the grieved place by the fire. I fancy the receipt much, for it standeth to good reason that a bird of Luna should help a disease of Saturn.

"*For procuring chastity*: Take the seeds of red nettle, beat them into powder and take a dram of it in white wine.

"*To increase the milk of nurses*: The hoofs of the forefeet of a cow dryed increaseth the milk of nurses, and the smoke of this, if burnt, driveth away mice."

It is interesting to note in many cases how some of our modern, up-to-date theories are hidden under Culpeper's extravagant precriptions—a kernel of truth wrapped, as it were, in a shell of fabulous conjecture. He tells us, for instance, that an admirable cure for consumption is—"to go in the country in sowing-time, and follow the plow, that so the sweet smell of the earth, newly broke up, may be taken into the nose; if this may not be, by reason of poverty or the season of the year, then let it suffice to go out into the field every morning and dig up a fresh turf and smell to it an hour or so together."

What could be more reasonable than his cure for obesity :

" Some men [he says] are so fat and gross that they can hardly walk or do any business. Let such eat two or three cloves of garlic to their breakfast and fast three hours afterwards and let them drink water wherein fennel hath been boiled and this will in a very short time ease them."

For fever Culpeper assures us that " cool and sweet air is essential," and after such good advice what does it matter that his sentence ends with " if the case be desperate, ye must apply pigeons to the soles of the feet."

One of the things that gives a peculiar charm to these extraordinary and rambling writings is the fact that a discerning reader will frequently come across passages that reveal the closest knowledge and observation of nature. Shakespeare's " Lady smock," or " Cuckoo flower," as it is now generally called, Culpeper records as being of " a blushing white colour," a description the exactness of which will not easily be lost upon anyone who has seen the flower growing in English pastures. In another place he refers to " the pools of water to be found in the holes and cleft roots of

129

beech-trees," and a little later he tells us that " each moss partakes of the nature of the tree from which it is taken." What a winning glimpse we have in the following entry of the old chemist pottering about over his specimens—" if the flower of cowslip be not well dried and kept in a warm place they will soon look green. If you let them see the sun once a month it will neither do the sun nor them any harm."

Listen, too, to his " cure for a lame beast." What an insight it gives one into the old superstitions of country life, such as we might imagine to be the natural mental background of the figures presented in some of George Morland's landscapes :

" If any beast, or horse, or kine be lame, mark where the lame or swelled foot doth stand and cut up a turf where the foot stood and hang it up if the weather be hot and dry on a white thorn, else in the chimney corner, and as fast as that dries the swelling will cease and the pain will go away."

During his life Culpeper wrote some seventy or more books. Many of these have been lost, some of them he left to

130

his wife, and others fell into the hands of an unscrupulous publisher. In the latter part of the seventeenth century there was a great demand for these volumes.

Nicholas Culpeper died in 1654. At the last this man of astrology and ancient lore was able as well as another to summon up his quota of faith. More sanguine than many a scholastic theologian, this old empiric, when owls' livers and bats' tongues were of no more avail, challenged death with the following brave assurance : " If I do die, I do but go out of a miserable world to receive a crown of immortality." May it have been so, and may he have been permitted by some divine dispensation to continue his beloved sciences in the Elysian fields, brewing out of the roots of asphodel and amaranth new herbal potations for the ghostly bodies of the heroic dead.

BEAU NASH

BEAU NASH

RICHARD NASH, despot of silk stockings and most tyrannical of beaux, was born at Swansea, 18th October 1674. His father was a small glass manufacturer, and in the days of his prosperity the incomparable dandy was wont to say, when twitted as to his reticence concerning his origin : " I seldom mention my father in company, not because I have any reason to be ashamed of him, but because he has some reason to be ashamed of me." Nash was educated at Oxford, where, in the words of Goldsmith, he showed " that though much might be expected from his genius, nothing could be hoped from his industry " ; indeed, it appears that he was compelled to absent himself from the university somewhat abruptly, leaving in his hastily abandoned chambers " some plays, a tobacco-box, and a fiddle."

After his unceremonious departure from Oxford, Nash occupied himself for the next few years ostensibly in reading law at the Inner Temple, though in reality

living " to the very edge of his finances "
as a man-about-town. In 1704 he betook
himself by stage-coach to Bath, a journey
which at that time was performed, " if
God permitted, in three days." Shortly
after his arrival, the Corporation of Bath
elected him Master of Ceremonies of that
city, a position which he held with eminent
success and unequalled pomp for more
than half-a-century.

It must not be thought that the post
was in any way a sinecure. It would
be difficult to enumerate all the varied
activities by which the debonair gamester
converted the humdrum West Country
town into the most fashionable centre of
eighteenth-century life in England. He
superintended the improving of the roads
leading to the city, had the streets lighted,
regulated the charges of the sedan-chair
men, had ballrooms and hospitals built,
and contrived suitable shelters round the
famous baths. Always an expert in such
matters as rank, precedence and urbane
decorum, he transformed the city of Bath
into a modish and exquisite resort for
gaming, foppery and gallantry.

When Beau Nash first took up office
his sense of the correct was considerably
136

exercised by a certain grossness of manners which prevailed at that time. It seems that in those days men were not at all ashamed to appear at polite gatherings in their jack-boots and the ladies in their aprons. As a counter-stroke to such unseemly practices Nash composed the following satirical rhyme :

" Come, trollops and slatterns,
Cockt hats and white aprons,
This best our modesty suits ;
For why should not we
In dress be as free
As Hogs-Norton 'squires in boots."

Nor was this his only method of displaying his displeasure. If Nash's eye so much as caught a glimpse of heavy footwear in an assembly-room, he would hurry across to the offender, and with a low bow inquire of him " if he had not forgotten his horse." Recalcitrant dames he would treat still more severely: on one occasion even going so far as to remove with his own hands, from the person of the Duchess of Queensberry, an apron of point-lace which was said to be worth five hundred guineas.

It was indeed a prim and elegant life

that Nash inaugurated, a life in which periwigged men of fashion, immaculate in all but their morals, strutted and minuetted before exquisitely patched and powdered ladies. They met at the pump-room, where they were diverted by the conversation of the " gay, the witty and the forward " ; they met at Spring Gardens, where on summer mornings they would tread a cotillion together on the smooth lawns between the painted flower-beds ; they met again as they made a tour " through the milliners and toymen, to stop at Mr Gill's, the pastrycook, to take a jelly, a tart, or a small basin of vermicelli." Each night they attended a ball opened with the minuet danced by a lady and gentleman " of the highest rank present " and followed by country dances " wherein the ladies according to their quality stood up first." At an appointed hour Nash would raise two fingers as a sign that it was time for the music to cease, and then, after a short interval for the dancers to cool, the company would take their departure.

What a delightful picture one gets of it all, of the sedate, pleasure-loving old town, with its abbey bells ringing out a

welcome to each fashionable arrival, with
Beau Nash hurrying down the cobbled
streets, his famous white beaver hat on
his head, to pay his compliments to each
new-comer. And what a gay figure he
himself must have cut in those resplendent
days ; indeed, we learn from Lord Chester-
field that his attire was on one occasion so
gorgeous " that as he stood by chance in
the midst of the dancers he was taken
by many to be a gilt garland." Though
Beau Nash was fond of declaring that
" Wit, flattery and fine clothes were
enough to debauch a nunnery," there is
little evidence that he himself ever indulged in intrigues with his fair visitors
who every morning like so many lovely
nymphs stepped into the elegant health-
giving waters and received from the hands
of their attendants " little floating dishes
into which to lay their handkerchiefs, little
nosegays and sweetmeats." Judging by
the standards of the eighteenth century,
it would seem that his personal life defied
criticism, for in an age " when a fellow
of high humour would drink no wine but
what was strained through his mistress's
smock," he can scarcely be condemned
for accepting the blandishments bestowed

139

upon him by his three successive adorers, Lady Betty Besom, Hannah Lightfoot and Juliana Popjoy.

An issue of *The Gentleman's Magazine* at the end of the eighteenth century throws a remarkable light upon the latter years of the last of these women. " Juliana Popjoy," it says, " died last week. For thirty or forty years she has lived in a hollow tree. She had been mistress to the famous Beau Nash of Bath."

In Wesley's *Journal* we find a curious description of a meeting that took place between that honest rantipole evangelist and Beau Nash. Wesley had come to hold a conventicle at Bath, which was, of course, the very stronghold of frivolity. Before his service opened, Nash appeared, and did not hesitate to protest that his preaching " frightened the people out of their wits."

" Sir, did you ever hear me preach?" inquired the Puritan of the Dandy.

" No," came the answer; " but I judge by common report."

" Common report, sir, is not enough. Give me leave, sir, to ask, is not your name Nash?"

" My name is Nash."

" Sir, I dare not judge of you by common

140

report." And with that, so the story runs, the man of fashion uttered not a word more, but walked silently away.

Are we to suppose that, as sometimes happens to simple souls, Beau Nash experienced at that moment a new and strange misgiving as to the import of the superficial existence which surrounded him and which in part he himself had been responsible for calling into existence? And is there perhaps some connection between his religious susceptibilities on that occasion and the extraordinary conduct of his lady in taking up her residence where patches and cosmetics were replaced by owls' pellets and bats' droppings?

Alas! as the years went by the evening of the Beau's life began to grow cloudy. The old man grew choleric and testy: he became egotistical, and would weary the company with his oft-repeated tales. There is something strangely pathetic about the spectacle of this aged " glass of fashion " clinging peevishly to the last remnants of his mock power, which with the passing of the years he had come to consider his natural right. " Old Beau Knash makes himself disagreeable to all who come to Bath. He is now become fit only to read

141

'Shirlock' upon death, by which he may save his soul and gaine more proffitts than ever he could by his white hatt, suppose it was to be dyed red," wrote an impertinent illiterate eager to usurp the old gentleman's place, who, having lived and prospered in the reigns of half-a-dozen sovereigns of England, was now "labouring under the unconquerable distemper of old age."

Sick and decrepit, the antique Macaroni drifted into poverty. At the last, even his cherished collection of snuff-boxes had to be sold, and he gladly accepted a pension of ten pounds to be delivered him on the first Monday of every month.

Only after his death did something of the glamour of his ancient renown revive. For we are told that on a certain afternoon in the middle of February, 1761, the farm-labourers of Somerset unyoked their oxen, the colliers ceased from mining, the weavers from spinning, in order to witness from the stately roof-tops of Bath the body of the celebrated old fop pass by on its way to its final resting-place in the abbey church; there to await the ordained hour when, in a form more glorified than it had ever been by lace or frill, it should be called to appear before the presence of its Maker.

142

JOHN WOOLMAN

JOHN WOOLMAN

O N certain rare occasions there have been men born whose dispositions are of so tender, so pure, so refined a nature, that, whether they will or no, in their sojourn through life, they find themselves constantly at odds with the accepted usages of this tough world. Such a man was Jesus of Nazareth; and St Francis of Assisi; and, with all reverence be it spoken, John Woolman of New Jersey.

The date of this great Quaker's birth was 1720, and for fifty-odd years he struggled manfully both by word and deed against everything in life that is gross, insensitive, uncivilised and wicked. It is perhaps doubtful, however, whether his efforts towards directing the steps of mankind into the paths " of pure wisdom " were quite as influential as his generous-hearted co-religionist, John Greenleaf Whittier, would have us believe. To many, the especial appeal of his writing is literary rather than social or religious, he being

one of those chaste spirits, like Thomas
à Kempis, like John Bunyan, like Boehme,
the pure fervour of whose souls is made
up of so sweet and transparent a temper
that their work, written for the devout
only, takes its place amongst the most
treasured volumes of the world's literature.

The forefront of an excellent and
exhaustive new edition of John Woolman
contains his picture; and as one looks at
the odd, woodcut-like features, so un-
couth, so homely, one is amazed to think
that this humble tradesman, by the simple
method of being true to himself, should
have won the affections of so many generations of men and women. " Get the writings
of John Woolman by heart and love the
early Quakers," wrote Charles Lamb in
the *Essays of Elia*; and there have been
many who have followed his advice, to their
infinite relish and edification. Again and
again, as we read the pages of his journal,
our complacence is touched to the quick.
In sentence after sentence, this common colonial tailor reveals a refinement
of nature, a gentleness of conscience, a
sanctity of thought which is as affecting
as certain of the more lovely and tragic
chapters of the New Testament. Indeed,

146

we can scarce peruse a single page of this book without feeling that our own sophisticated reactions are altogether obtuse beside the direct, unaffected goodness of this simple man.

He is not one to be deceived about evil, though it be disguised never so subtly in " deep-rooted custom." For example, he goes into the Southern States and is sorely " exercised " over the condition of the slaves there. His lively imagination envisages at once the iniquity of the trade, sees these wretched human beings " bound with thongs and heavily laden with elephants' teeth " passing from their forest homes to the sea. Because the Southern States especially were involved in fostering the abominable trade, it seemed to him that " a dark gloominess is hanging over the Land." " In future, the consequence will be grievous to posterity," he declares. " Many slaves on this continent are oppressed," he says simply, and goes on to assure us, with the utmost confidence, that " their cries have reached the ears of the Most High." It might perhaps prove a difficult task to test the accuracy of the latter statement, but that their cries reached the ears of John Woolman there can be small doubt. From year to year " he laboured with the disobedient, laying things home and close to such who were stout against the truth." Nor was it the condition of the slaves only that roused his sympathy; his interests extended to the Red Indians also. There is something extremely affecting about his missionary journey to this ill-fated race. " The thought of falling into the hands of Indian warriors was," he confesses, " in times of weakness afflicting to me." And yet, in spite of the fact that news had just come in of " slain and scalped English people from the Fort called Pittsburg," we find him persisting in his hazardous under-taking, being fortunately " preserved by him whose works in these Mountain Deserts appeared awful." It is quite clear that, in his relations with nature, John Woolman never felt wholly at ease. He found difficulty in sleeping out of doors and, on more than one occasion, when the " mosquetoes were pleanty," he perforce would spend long hours looking up at the stars and contemplating " the condition of our first parents." Violent activity of any kind was extremely antipathetic to John Woolman's sober nature. When he

148

saw, on certain large forest trees (which had been peeled for the purpose), primitive drawings representing the military exploits of the Indians, " the desire to cherish the spirit of love and peace amongst this people, arose very fresh in me"; and this feeling became more and more strengthened in him as he considered " the toyls and fatigues of warriors . . . and of their business and great weariness in chasing one another over the Rocks and Mountains and of the restless unquiet state of most of those who live in this spirit."

What charming revelations he makes concerning his own personal life with Sarah Ellis, his wife—that " well-enclined damsel." The natural sorrows which beset his days he puts down each in its place. He carefully records, for instance, the death of his sister Elizabeth, a Quakeress of the kind that Charles Lamb likens to a " lily," whose last, sweet and incredible confession sounds still, after all these years, so infinitely touching: " When I was a young girl I was wanton and airy."

As quite a young man, John Woolman makes an avowal of that open secret, the understanding of which contributes so much to happiness in this world. " I saw that a humble man, with the Blessing of the Lord, might live on a little." He perceived that most people were " too much cloged with the things of this life," seeing that merchandise is " attended with much care and cumber." Whenever, therefore, his own business showed signs of prospering unduly, he felt a " stop in my mind " and a strong inclination to " live according to pure wisdom and cease from any inordinate desire after wealth." He even went so far as to advise his customers to go elsewhere, whereby he was delivered from " the entangling expenses of a curious, delicate, luxurious life " and felt himself free to repair to his own apple-yard where he would spend " a good deal of time howing, grafting, trimming and inoculating."

What a lovable figure he must have presented in his orchard, as he busied himself with his pruning-knife, his quaint, woodcut, God-intoxicated head " covered with a hat the natural colour of the fur " ! The purchasing of this hat had at one time exercised him much. For years he had felt scruples against wearing any dyed articles, and yet had been equally " apprehensive of being looked upon as one affecting

singularity." He has given us the sequel
of the matter in his own delightful words:
" While that Singularity was only for His
sake, on this account I was under close
exercise of mind in the time of our General
Spring meeting 1762 . . . being then
deeply bowed in Spirit before the Lord,
was made willing to speak for a Hat of
the natural colour of fur (and did so)."
It would seem that his misgivings had not
been altogether without foundation, for
he tells us significantly that there were
those who " carried shy of me."

As the years passed, his over-susceptible
conscience grew more and more punctilious.
Towards the end of his life, when he made
his " floating pilgrimage " to England, he
refused to travel anywhere but in the
steerage, asserting that the unnecessary
ornamentation expended on the cabins
would have been sufficient to give the poor
sailors better quarters. Though he held
stoutly to the opinion that " a communica-
tion from one part of the world to some
other part of it, by sea, is at times consistent
with the will of our Heavenly Father," he
is seriously preoccupied over the unhappy
state of the lads trained as seamen. Indeed,
so refined had his sympathies become at

this time, that he felt considerable concern for the very "dunghill fowls" which he observed to abstain from crowing from the moment they left the Delaware till they sighted the coast of Cornwall. When he considered "the dull appearance and pineing sickness of some of them," he was conscious of a care that should be felt in us "that we do not lessen that Sweetness of life in the animal creation," and became strongly convinced "that a less number carried off to eat at Sea may be more agreeable to the pure wisdom."

He reached England only to encounter fresh moral agitations : "So great is the hurry in the Spirit of the world . . . that Creation at this day doth loudly groan ! . . . Stage Coaches frequently go up-wards a hundred miles in twenty-four hours . . . the horses be killed with hard driving and many others are driven till they are blind."

John Woolman of New Jersey was not the man to be party to such abominations, so we find him setting out for the north of England on foot, in which harmless wayfaring "the sight of innocent birds in the branches and sheep in the pastures, who are according to the will of the Creator, hath at times tended to mitigate my trouble."

At York he fell sick of the smallpox, and a few days later he died. He left instructions "not to have his Coffin made of Oak, because it is a wood more useful than ash for some other purposes." "I look at the Face of my dear Redeemer, for Sweet is his voice and his Countenance Comely," were his last words; and surely we are justified in surmising that if ever mortal man reached that "pure habitation" which, he himself assures us, "God has prepared for his servants," that man was John Woolman.

THOMAS BEWICK

THOMAS BEWICK

ON the bookshelves of almost all English houses which possess country traditions one can make sure of finding editions of Bewick's *Birds* and *Quadrupeds*. The three volumes may not often be taken down, but there they are ready to hand should ever an uncommon bird or animal make its appearance. Old-fashioned people are particularly fond of these books; one fancies they find the actual name " Bewick " reassuring, the very sight and sound of it, so essentially English. Their instinct is perfectly right, for when one looks again at these famous engravings they do seem to express in a most exact and intimate way the particular romance, if we may call it so, which we associate in our minds with the English countryside.

This romance is not easy to define, possibly it can be appreciated only by people who have lived all their lives in the country. It has to do with the indefinable delight and relish of the long-drawn-out seasons which they have known from childhood;

it has to do with the very smell of the damp
autumn air when there is continual dripping from the bare branches on to coloured
leaves—with the very tang of frosty
mornings when the first cat's-ice is upon
the roads—with the bite in the air when
the weather-vanes are pointing north-east
for days together, and the water in tanks
and butts is solid ice: it is what gives
to so many wayside objects, such as milestones and sign-posts, that wistful, almost
articulate, look—causing one to fancy
that they cannot have been altogether
oblivious of the generations which have
passed them by.

In reading the early chapters of Bewick's
autobiography one at once recognises the
influences which helped to develop his
homely earthbound genius. He was often
present, he tells us, "at the worrying of
foxes and foumarts and otters and badgers,"
and would go "to the sheep on the fells
through wreaths of snow, with a bundle
of hay on his back and his pocket full of
oats." He liked to sit by the fireside in
the late evenings listening to old North
Country stories and memories of folk dead
long ago, "whose lot it was useless to sigh,
the winds having blown over their graves

158

for many ages past." As a small boy he had a mania for drawing; he would work with a piece of chalk in the church porch at Ovingham and on the hearthstone of his home, often, so he tells us, " scorching his face " there when the fire was more than usually hot. At fourteen he was apprenticed to an engraver in Newcastle, and for the next five years was employed in engraving coffin-plates and the brass faces of grandfather clocks, occupations one imagines curiously coinciding with the natural bent of his thought, as we have come to know it in his woodcuts. When the time came for him to set out for Newcastle it was, he writes, " with bitter sadness " that he said good-bye " to Mickley Bank, Stubcross, the whinney wilds, the woods, rivers, and especially to the old hollow elm which had sheltered the salmon fishers from many a bitter blast." But he often revisited his home, walking to Cherryburn, " which for many years my eyes have beheld with *cherished delight* . . . with its holy hedge, and well, and two ash-trees grown from the same root."

" I thought nothing in those days of leaving Newcastle at seven o'clock on a

159

winter's evening, the worst that fell from the sky never deterred me from taking a journey. To be placed in the midst of a wood in the night, in a whirlwind of snow, while the blasts howled above my head was sublimity itself."

One hardly wonders, after reading this, that travellers battling against the elements in their wayfaring is a recurring theme of his tail-pieces: with their antique hats, their hedge-sticks, and their old clouts about them, they make their way along a thousand windswept, rain-drenched roads.

As soon as his apprenticeship was over he returned to his father at Cherryburn. It was at this time that he went walking half across Scotland. In his realistic way he tells us how the idea of the tramp first came to him. "When fishing on a hot day in June, I suddenly gave up and laying down my rod awhile, I then tied it up, and walked home: having resolved to see more of the country, I requested my mother to put up some shirts, sewed three guineas in my breeches' waistband and set off that afternoon and walked to Haydon Bridge."

In 1776 he went to London for a year,

160

but he has little good to say for the place:
one suspects him of spending most of his
time in the " Hole in the Wall " with his
North Country friends. In 1784 his father
and mother died, the former on 15th
November, which, as the old egoist quaintly
records, was the very day on which he began
the business " of cutting the blocks with
the figure of a dromedary " for his book
of *Quadrupeds*. The book was published
in 1790 and was an immediate success.
The first volume of *Birds* appeared in 1797
and the second in 1804.

The subjects he chose for his engravings
are for the most part of the earth earthy.
They are blunt, direct and shrewd, and
many of them could hardly be called
" genteel," to use a phrase of his time.
They give one the impression of being
never far removed from the ploughed fields
and honest mud of Northumberland. No
one in quite the same way as Bewick has
entered into the rude habits and instincts
of people who live in direct contact with
the soil. It would seem that he derived a
peculiar satisfaction from portraying them
in all their roughness and uncouthness.

Clodhoppers, drunkards, gluttons, such
are the folk he so often catches in some

161

careless, unconscious moment to perpetu-
ate for ever: a fat, gross farmer in his
cellar, the spigot out of the barrel, and he
too drunk to stop the flow of liquor; a
drunk man lying insensible at the roadside.
He likes also scenes which indicate callous-
ness and savagery in man or beast; a stray
dog limping off and three men after it with
gun and sticks; a forgotten sheep nibbling
at the twigs of a broom outside a deserted,
snow-covered mountain hut; a cat in a
tub drifting out to sea, the wretched
creature on its hind legs peering into the
water, its cottage home still just in sight
on the shore, and darkness coming on.
All the untoward accidents and quaint
happenings of village life afford an ample
field for his craft; a blind old man saying
his grace and a cat the while stealing his
porridge; an eager sportsman coming
down to the river-side after a bird he has
shot, the wounded bird escaping unseen
by an overhanging bank; a man tracking
a hare in the snow, the animal, small as a
pin's head, crossing a field in the distance;
a traveller by moonlight nervously peering
into a darkened recess by the roadside,
the place full of shadowy goblins.

Many of these pictures have for their

162

motive the transitory nature of things upon earth : it would seem that Bewick's mind was abnormally conscious of this. The idea evidently haunted him. " All things flow away, nothing remains "; he could never rid his old North Country head of this melancholy conception. Like the writing on a sundial, Bewick's engravings are never weary of reminding us that " Life is a shadow." Ruined churches, forgotten tombstones, tottering monuments appealed to the old rogue's humour better than anything; he likes to engrave the flat slabs with such words as " *Firmum in vita nihil,*" " *Vanitas vanitatum omnia vanitas.*" Thus he will draw a monument " erected to commemorate a splendid victory " and have a donkey rubbing its backside against it and all so exquisitely done that one can imagine that one sees the animal's grey hairs coming off on the moss-grown surface.

But possibly the most original of all his vignettes is placed at the foot of the page describing the Kingfisher. It is in Bewick's best mood and style and would be recognised anywhere as his handiwork—a man is seen walking at night-time in the direction of a distant church, a full moon is in the sky, on the man's back is a black kite-shaped burden which on closer scrutiny is seen to be a coffin inscribed with the words: " A wonderful fish." When one observes that this picture is placed under the Kingfisher, and is evidently intended to remind us of another kind of fishing which daily takes place under the sun, one is given to marvel at the grim attitude of this Newcastle tradesman in the face of happenings which, when clearly understood, have made many wiser men quail.

Bewick died in 1828. The very last tail-piece he did was of a coffin being carried from Cherryburn down to the Tyne, where a moored boat is waiting to bear the dead body of Thomas Bewick across the water.

WILLIAM BARNES

WILLIAM BARNES

"GOOD for the bider, bad for the rider," such was the curt, homely proverb by which the country people of Wessex in mediæval times used to describe the heavy, rich, alluvial soil from which they derived their livelihood. Indeed there can be found no meadows throughout the length and breadth of England more opulent than those of Dorsetshire, and in Dorset itself none richer than those that are situated in the fertile valley of Blackmore, within the green margins of which William Barnes, the dialect poet, passed his life.

He was born in 1800 and died in 1886, and during this long span of years was scarcely ever out of earshot of that broad-mouthed speech, " the bold, broad Doric of England," which, as it pleased him to remember, was derived almost without change from the " Eald Seaxan." Just as the great spreading oaks and trimmed or " shrouded " elms grow indigenous and sturdy from the fecund soil of those

167

favoured acres, so is it with his dialect poetry. Every verse, every line of it, seems to have been bathed in those lovely blue mists of dawn, " the pride of the morning," as the village people call them, which during the earlier hours of the long days of summer so frequently envelop the hedgerow trees.

William Barnes was a man of old-fashioned tastes and habits. Up to the day of his death he was accustomed to wear the eighteenth-century dress. Thomas Hardy gives us this delightful glimpse of him :

" Few figures were more familiar to the eye in the county town of Dorset on a market day than an aged man, quaintly attired in capel cloak, knee breeches, and buckled shoes, with a leather satchel slung over his shoulders and a stout staff in his hand. . . . Every Saturday morning he might be seen trudging up the narrow South Street of Dorchester . . . till he reached the four crossways. Halting here opposite the public clock, he would pull his old-fashioned watch from its deep fob and set it with great precision to London time."

Bagbere, the little hamlet where William Barnes was born, is situated on the banks

of the River Stour, and his poetry is almost
entirely concerned with the fields, home-
steads, straw-strewn bartons and grassy
honeysuckle lanes that are within walking
distance of that most lovely river. Indeed
there are many people who find it difficult
to dissociate his poetry from its slowly
moving waters : waters whose muddy
bottoms have from the earliest days given
such good harbourage to the coarser kinds
of fish ; to eels and leather-mouthed chub,
and red-dorsal-finned roach. Of all English rivers, the River Stour is the most
friendly. Along under its sweet alder-
shaded pools no danger ever lurks ; no
evil undercurrents ever disturb its wide,
cider-coloured reaches, as by wood and
" drong," by park and flowering meadow,
it winds its way towards the Channel, with
no other purpose, it would seem, than to
fill with good Stour milk the heavy udders
of the dairy cows that frequent the margins
of its glimmering levels, where, all day
long, over the flat water-lily leaves, dragon-
flies, red and blue, hover aslant.

Within this gentle environment all
that is old, all that is time-worn, all that
has been made sacred by human association, inspires the response of the poet :

169

the church bells that swing in belfries
where the timber is dusty with the dust of
centuries—

" An' frettèn worms ha' slowly wound,
  Droo beams the wold vo'k lifted sound "

—the door-posts of the cottages that have
been chafed smooth by so many goings-
out and comings-in; the very farm wains
whose painted shafts have had upon them
the mud of so many winters, the fine pollen
dust of so many summers.

In his poetry there can be found no
trace of that black salt of disillusionment,
bitter to the taste as the milk of dandelions
or the roots of certain weeds, that seems
to have become so inseparable from the
work of the poets of these latter years.
Never for one single moment does he
suspect the world of concealing for human
life yawning gaps and ghastly insecurities!
Nothing but what may be called " natural
sorrows " ever darkens the brows of the
simple folk whom he portrays from the
time when, as swaddled children, they are
held over the " hallowed stone " of the
baptismal font till the hour when their
bones are laid to rest amongst those of

their fathers and of the old men before them.

What if the greater part of his poetry is made up of a mere record of the varying loveliness of the passing seasons, as in recurring procession they adorn and lay bare again the ancient Wessex soil? Is it not the employment of just this faculty of unaffected poetic observation that is the very breath of consciousness to people who spend their lives in close proximity to nature?

How surely Barnes catches those vague intimations of an inexpressible beauty which trouble us anew at the coming of each spring and which are never more poignantly felt than when, on some early April morning, the " charm " of the birds, louder than could have been conceived, breaks in upon the senses of the country sleepers, lying under their coloured quilts in whitewashed cottage rooms, down in the West Country ! With equal ease he recovers the very sense of magical seclusion that falls upon the midnight pastures of Dorset, where, far from the hum of cities, " the sight o' cows asleep in glittrèn dew " can intoxicate the soul with an anguish of ecstasy almost greater than can be borne.

No one, not even Hardy, can conjure

up more surely the picture of a sweltering hayfield at the time of the Feast of St Barnabas : the hard-working labourers, " Wi' their eärms in white sleves, left an' right," the glittering farm instruments, the swathes of wilting, sweet-smelling grass, the slow-worms, the mice, the little green, cold-backed frogs :

" Or in the day, a-vleèn drough
    The leafy trees, the whoa'se gookoo
    Do zing to mowers that do zet
    Their zives on end, an' stan' to whet."

Again, in the following lines, has he not conveyed the exact impression of an opulent dairy-land when the first burst of June is over ?—

" I came along, where wide-horn'd cows
    Ithin a nook, ascreen'd by boughs
    Did stan' an flip the white-hooped pails
    Wi' häiry tufts o' swingèn tails."

In half-a-dozen words he is often able to do what with another poet would take as many pages !

" Where cows did slowly seek the brink
    O'Stour, drough zunburnt grass, to
        drink."

To a West Country man these lines bring back in a single flash the very look of the familiar sun-bleached meadows when, from the white, gull-haunted cliffs of St Albans Head to the Mendips that overlook Glastonbury, they lie prostrate under an August sun. How unmistakably, how essentially English the old man's poems are !—like clods dug up from an East Chaldon mead, smelling of primroses and daisies and damp island-mould. How delightful is his half-humorous belief in fairies, which takes us back once more to the snoring ploughman, the dreaming, moonlit parks, the enamelled snake-skins, acorn cups and cowslip-freckles of Shakespeare's homely imagination. When William Barnes, wandering through autumn fields, looked at the haws in the hedgerows, they were " pixie pears " to him, and the toadstools under the sodden, moss-grown beech-tree roots were " pixie stools." In one of his poems two rustics hold discourse over one of those mysterious circles of rough herbage which one still comes upon in the grass of the immemorial acres that lie under the shadow of the grey, squat tower of Milton Abbey :

" ' But in the daytime where do veäries
    hide?
Where be their hwomes, then? Where do
    veäries bide?'
' Oh! they do get away down under
    ground
In hollow pleäzen where they can't be
    vound.' ''

Old words, old ditties, old, childish in-
cantations are all dear to him. He likes
to record how the children at play in the
overgrown gardens of his favourite valley
sing in mocking tones to the grey-white
" puss moths " that they catch :

    " Millery, millery, dousty pole !
      How many zacks hast thee a-stole
      Vour and twenty in a peck
      Hang the miller up by's neck."

Or again :

" How we—when nettles had a-stung
Our little hands, when we wer young—
Did rub em wi' a dock, an' zing
Out nettl', in dock. In dock, out sting."

The very look and character of certain
places in Dorset he can bring before the

174

eyes of her exiled sons with heart-breaking vividness :

" At Stalbridge, wi' its grey-wall'd park."

" Sweet Be'minster, that bist-abound
  By green an' woody hills all round."

Or with unfaltering craft he will etch in little intimate glimpses of country matters as living and realistic as the woodcuts of Thomas Bewick :

" An' ho'ses there wi' lwoads of grist
  Do stand an' toss their heavy heads."

" A yellow-banded bee did come,
  An' softly pitch, wi' hushèn hum
  Upon a beän, an' there did sip,
  Upon a swäyèn blossom's lip."

" An' I do zee the friskèn lams
  Wi swingèn tails an' wooly lags
  A-playèn roun' their veedèn dams
  An' pullèn o' their milky bags."

In many of his poems, also, we come upon the expression of that sturdy devotion for the actual soil out of which they have sprung, which time and again has enabled the simple folk of the West " to show the

mettle of their pastures " in England's hour
of need :

" We Do'set, though we mid be hwomely
    Be'nt asheamed to own our pleäce
And we've zome women not uncomely
    Nor asheämed to show their feäce :
We've a meäd or two wo'th mowèn
We've an ox or two wo'th showèn
    In the village,
    At the tillage,
Come along an' you shall vind
That Dorset men don't sheäme their kind.

The primrwose in the sheäde do blow,
    The cowslip in the zun,
The thyme upon the down do grow,
    The clote where streams do run ;
An' where do pretty maidens grow
An' blow, but where the tow'r
    Do rise among the bricken tuns,
    In Blackmwore by the Stour."

In his power of portraying the pathos
inherent in the transitory nature of all
things human he may be said to rival
Wordsworth. He understood only too
well the sorrow of a man for the woman
he has lost, or of a mother for her child,
amongst a people whose deep natures are

not easily to be comforted. It is said that he himself for nearly forty years wrote down each day in his journal the name of his dead wife. Any familiar material objects that seem to suggest at least a relative permanence are always sufficient to put his mind into a mood of sweet melancholy; a turnstile perhaps, at the end of a field path, which has swung its white arms a thousand times to let pass a beloved one who never again, either in March or November, will go by that way; or, it may be, a spreading oak-tree whose knotted bark in three-score years and ten has scarce added six inches to its enormous girth. Such deep-rooted meditations find an easy utterance in the mellow vernacular, made up not of " hard words," as the village people of Dorset call King's English, but of a language whose broad phrases would seem indeed to have had their origin in the heart rather than in the head.

Reading the poetry of William Barnes is like listening to an old-fashioned grace or to the singing which Izaak Walton heard on the banks of the Thames. In one of his small prose works there is a passage that has always seemed to me to express most happily the natural piety of his mind.

There is about it something of the pure, unaffected beauty that belongs to certain sentences in the works of Oliver Goldsmith :

" I had been working in my garden. The sun was just below the horizon and the dew was already on the smooth green walks bordered by sweet-smelling roses and carnations. The stillness of the evening was broken only by the whistling of a blackbird. I sat down on a rude seat I had formed beneath an old tree and, as I thought of the fruits and plants that were ripening around me, I exclaimed to myself, ' How happy if they knew it, are they that till the ground.' "

William Barnes died in a small hamlet near Dorchester ; and it is in that old county town that a statue of him may be seen, at the foot of which one may read this verse, taken from his poem to the good Squire of Culver Dell :

" But now I hope his kindly feäce
    Is gone to vind a better pleäce,
    But still wi' vok a' left behind
    He'll always be a-kept in mind."

It stands, this image of a man in whose heart no guile was to be found, confronting

178

the familiar high street, along which he had
so often made his way amid the clamour
of folk and beasts come in to market from
the fields and grounds he knew and loved
so well.

THOMAS HARDY

THOMAS HARDY

THE ancient oak-trees of the Blackmore Vale have burst into summer leaf more than eighty times since that morning in early June when a plain country woman—the wife of a Dorset workman—gave birth to Thomas Hardy. The novelist's first glimpse of the earth was the rain-drenched hayfields that surround Bockhampton, and surely never since the birth of Shakespeare has there been born an English poet whose art is more dependent upon the actual soil of the English shires. For Thomas Hardy writes like a countryman, thinks like a countryman, and has the imagination of a countryman. From first to last the essential element of the drama of existence has been for him nothing more than the simple spectacle of mortal man and mortal woman, passionate and bewildered, moving against a background of immemorial nature. Hardy's eye can see beneath the mechanical structures of the modern city, beneath its girders and stone pilasters, beneath its hard, flat pavements to the very slag and soil which lies below. His is the deep, shrewd outlook of an old shepherd whose native observations of life and death have supplied him with a tough, idiosyncratic, earth-bound philosophy.

With Hardy there is none of that itching love of propaganda that mars the work of so many of our present-day writers. Changes in the organisation of society possess little interest for him, seeing that they are incapable of taking from the heart of man one jot of the ache of love, one tittle of the dolour of the recurring tragedy of death. This, to be sure, is a simple fact and one easily to be conned by " a man of measuring eye," who on a summer evening at Stalbridge or Sturminster-Newton listens to the voices of the girls and boys as they loiter together, or who, in meditative mood, surveys the grass-grown mounds, so solitary, so remote, that gather themselves year by year about the old churches of those two most lovely places.

In his admirable little book on the Wessex poet Professor Chew has observed how the enthusiasm aroused by the Wessex novels retarded for many years Hardy's

184

recognition as a poet. With its mania for cataloguing genius, the careless public was at first content to know that a new master of imaginative prose had appeared, and it required nearly three decades of accumulated testimony to establish in the general mind the value of his poetry. Yet this extraordinary verse, gouged out, word for word, line by line, from the very interstices of Hardy's mental structure, has about it an idiosyncratic and twisted authenticity expressive of the very soul of the man's originality. These poems are like knotted hedge-sticks, like ancient bell-hammers, like odd pieces of cottage furniture, or like the worm-eaten timber from a village bier that has borne away the corpses of a score of generations. Such entire possession do they take of their subject that they suggest the idea that the words have been put into position by hand. It is as though to this son of a mason the words had actually the semblance of stones and consequently called for the same vigorous and deliberate manner of treatment. Sometimes by the use of some goblin-quaint expression, sometimes by merely an unfamiliar transposition, Hardy's simplest lines are stamped with his unmistakable and indelible mark:

185

" When mid-autumn moan shook the night-time."

" Since the viands were out-set here."

" That the vows of men and maids are frail and fitful mouthings mere."

" And surceased in the sky, and but left in the gloaming.
Sea mutterings and me."

" A thinker of crooked thoughts upon Life in the sere."

Yet from out of these rugged creations there comes from time to time a music as wistful and heart-breaking as ever was the noise of falling rain in a deserted summer garden. Take, for example, the lovely refrain of Tess's Lament :

" I would that folk forgot me quite,
　　Forgot me quite !
I would that I could shrink from sight,
　　And no more see the sun."

Or the scarcely less plaintive reverie of Marty South :

" We work here together
In winter's breeze ;
He fills the earth in, I hold the trees.

From the bundle at hand here
I take each tree
And set it to stand, here
Always to be ;
When, in a second
As if from fear
Of life unreckoned
Beginning here,
It starts a sighing
Through day and night
Though while down lying
'Twas voiceless quite."

It will be noticed that one of the favourite occupations of Hardy's genius is this very power of imparting to the dim consciousness of lives other than human his own sombre reactions. In so natural and unaffected a way does he achieve this that the birds of the air, the furred animals of the fields, the trees and leaves and flowers seem to be uttering, year in and year out, a strange undertone of doleful protest against all " terrestrial happenings." Consider, for instance, the kind of superconsciousness displayed in the poem called *An August Midnight*, in which the poet compares his own musings with the instinctive knowledge that is possessed by

187

the five quaint insects that, attracted by the light of his lamp, have invaded his study.

Like some ubiquitous ghost the brooding mind of Hardy is here and there and everywhere. Now it is near the Pulpit Rock at the end of Portland Bill listening to the souls of the Wessex dead as they whir their way homewards, now at the top of the hill on the Blandford Road listening to what Yellham Woods have to say, and now still and pensive in the great nave of Salisbury Cathedral. What a devotion he shows for the West Country, for the places, rural usages, and all that rich and indiscriminate legacy from past ages which is its fortunate heritage. The individual milestones " by fosse-way field, and turnpike tracks " seem to be known by him, their particular shape, their weather-beaten appearance, and the quarries from which each of them was hewn so many centuries ago; he seems to know every thatched dormered window that opens upon the Vale of Avalon, and every old-fashioned, mouse-haunted mill under whose raftered cellars the slow-moving waters of the Parret, Yeo, or Stour splash and gurgle their way to the sea.

It is consoling to think how hard a task

it would be to present Hardy's writings in any conventional form. In verse after verse this sad-eyed Prometheus of the Dorset meadows sends out his challenge against the President of the Immortals :

" Crass Casualty obstructs the sun and rain
   And dicing Time for gladness casts a moan."

  " Has some Vast Imbecility
    Mighty to build and blend
    But impotent to tend
    Framed us in jest and left us now to hazardry ? "

  " He sank to raptness, as of yore,
    And opening New Year's Day
    Wove it by rote as theretofore
    And went on working evermore
    In his unweeting way."

In his appreciation of *The Dynasts*, Professor Chew speaks of the epic as " rising to majestic heights when the subject inspires it," but, quite apart from such " inspired " passages, the drama often attains a high level in the Shakespearean raciness of its more simple scenes. What could

189

be better than the loyal West Country man's misgivings lest King George III.. while staying at Weymouth, should be snapped up by Bonaparte, "like a minnow by a her'n"? How excellent is that ditty sung by the boatmen and longshoremen in the tavern by the backwater, that song which describes the storm after Trafalgar as it was felt at home by the seafaring folk who dwell in the little white stone houses, "with doors blocked with sand," that cluster about the Chesil beach. The words truly carry with them the very smell of those forlorn windswept habitations with their fishing-tackle and pitch; the very taste of the salt fresh rain, as it comes slanting down against the small windows that have for a view the engulfing watery grey wastes of the Atlantic.

Was ever the feeling of nostalgia expressed in a more intimate and natural way than by the drunken English deserter who, as he lies hidden in the straw of a ruined house in Spain, begins to long to be back in England?—"Ay, at home aleaning against Bristol Bridge and no questions asked, and the winter sun slanting friendly over Baldwin Street as 'a used to do."

The picture of the arrival of the mail-

190

coach at Durnover with the news of
Napoleon's escape from Elba is presented
with astonishing vividness. We see it all
—the mud-stained coach being skidded
while the sweating horses stale, the parson
with his long pipe, and the Dorset rustics
agape as they gaze first at the postilions
and then at their burning effigy of
the " little corporal " whose smouldering
" innerds " have been proved in very truth
to be " but a lock of straw from Bridle's
Barton."

In what an amazing way Hardy reveals
the secrets of the ancient and historic
landscape that is so dear to him. He makes
" the drowthy downlands " alive with
butterflies, and fills our nostrils with the
heavy odour of the dripping, antique farm-
yard cider-presses. Small wonder that in
one poem he conceives himself as being
remembered after he is dead not as " meta-
physician, bard," but as one who had an
intimate love of all country things, a love
of the hedgehogs that on dreaming summer
nights were wont to move across the lawn
at Max Gate, a love of the recurring sound
of the church bells as the wind in fitful
gusts carried their music from Dorchester
or the valley of the Frome, and a love of

the heavenly constellations as they came up out of the waters of the English Channel and went down again behind High Stoy and the hills that overlook the manors, woods and pastures of the Blackmore Vale.